Become
Truly Great

Become Truly Great

Serve the Common Good Through

Management by Positive Organizational Effectiveness

Charles G. Chandler

Published by Author Academy Elite
P.O. Box 43, Powell, OH 43065 (USA)
www.AuthorAcademyElite.com

Library of Congress control number: 2016962865
Softcover: ISBN 978-1-946114-27-3
Hardcover: ISBN 978-1-946114-28-0

Available in hardcover, softcover, Kindle, e-pub, and audiobook editions

To my parents, Charlie and Nita Chandler

CONTENTS

Part I:
The Present Age of 'Efficiencyism'

Part II:
The Coming Age of Organizational Effectiveness

Part III:
Entering the Age of Organizational Effectiveness

LIST OF FIGURES

PROLOGUE

There has been a long-standing puzzle in management theory. It revolves around a simple question: "What is organizational effectiveness?" Over the years, several answers have been proposed, but none has solved the puzzle. The problem is that theory does not point to anything specific that can be observed in the real world to verify effectiveness. Scholars call it a 'referent'; profit doesn't work, shareholder value doesn't work, a myriad of other organizational indicators fail to signify effectiveness in a way that would satisfy the puzzle — because these cannot be observed directly in the field. Scholars have been at an impasse in this area since the mid-1980s. Thus, 'effectiveness' has been called an enigma and a wicked problem, and remains a vague *construct* rather than a defined *concept* in organization and management theory.

If we don't know how to define organizational effectiveness, there is a good chance that we don't understand organizations. It is important that we do. Organizations have a central role in modern life. They offer goods and services. They are places to work. They regulate our economy. They are force multipliers, allowing individuals to achieve purposes much larger than they could accomplish by themselves. The best organizations help add meaning to our lives. In short, organizations are enablers of civilization, and creators of economic wealth and social capital. Truly great organizations occupy an important niche in their environment, and act in ways that benefit the common good.

Yet, it will come as no surprise that many organizations are ineffective in business, government, or non-profit sectors today. While they may have a vision of a better future, their efforts to bring it about have gained little traction. Ineffective organizations become marginalized, while other, more effective organizations achieve significant impact around them. Ineffectiveness has a significant downside. It can call into question the survival of an organization, not to mention the dysfunction and confusion experienced by the people inside. Ineffective organizations do little good for themselves or for the world around them.

Without an accepted theory that explains organizational effectiveness, confusion reigns. It colors the way that management theory is taught in business schools, and management is practiced by C-suite executives. It pervades the way politicians make policy, and citizens think about government. It holds us back from achieving a sustainable future.

A story is emerging about the need for organizations to enter a new age, one that this book calls The Age of Organizational Effectiveness. There are several threads to the story. One recounts the difficult situation that society finds itself in on multiple fronts, with limited options, and no clear path forward. Another thread is about widespread dissatisfaction with what capitalism has now become. Another is about the prevalence of 'efficiencyism,' which holds organizations back from realizing their true potential. It is also about other voices that have tried, but have not found a clear way ahead.

This book offers a path to the new age. The approach described herein was generated from a belief that a solution to the enigma of effectiveness can be found to satisfy both scholars and practitioners. It comes in the form of a new synthesis of organizational effectiveness theory (provided herein by the author) which not only defines a practical concept of effectiveness for the first time, but offers a deeper understanding of the nature of organizations themselves.

The Age of Organizational Effectiveness can arrive when managers begin to "think different," and implement the principles of effectiveness – one organization at a time. The world needs great organizations, and positive organizational effectiveness is the engine of greatness. Society now faces myriad problems that only truly great organizations can solve together by serving the common good. Welcome to Management by Positive Organizational Effectiveness.

INTRODUCTION

This book is about a new way to think about and manage organizations — whether business, government, or non-profit. It explains how to become truly great by serving the common good (i.e., the external environment). It has been written for practitioners, that is, managers and organizational leaders, but scholars will appreciate that its arguments are founded upon a new synthesis of theory. The approach is called Management by Positive Organizational Effectiveness (M+OE). Importantly, it can be applied to all types of organizations. It can also be applied when loose coalitions of organizations work together toward a common purpose (e.g., to save the world). Management by Positive Organizational Effectiveness provides a way to achieve great things.

There are three phases to Management by Positive Organizational Effectiveness: 1) Be Virtuous, 2) Discover Effectiveness, and 3) Become Truly Great. At first, you may think that too much is being promised. Doesn't it strain credulity to think that organizations can become great by following a simple formula? Well, no. There is little day-light between being virtuous, discovering effectiveness, and becoming great. The book puts tools at your disposal; naturally, the outcomes and impacts depend on how you use the tools, and on what response you receive in the real world. While worthwhile journeys are seldom completed without difficulty, persistence is often rewarded. You probably knew that already. Nevertheless, the book is designed to help those who have set their sights on greatness, by making the path less arduous.

In Phase 1, you are invited to start your journey toward greatness by examining whether your organization is virtuous. This may seem puzzling. It should not be. Even drug cartels can manage effective organizations, so it is important to apply super powers for good rather than evil. Think of Google's admonition to itself, "don't be evil." Yet the approach goes beyond simple slogans. Phase 1 of M+OE is about instilling positive values in your organization that can both attract and amplify success, while being protective on the road ahead. Positive values and attributes such as honesty, decency, transparency, high quality, resource conservation, and doing what's best for the customer need to be guaranteed within your processes because internal behaviors matter. It is important to do this at the beginning of the journey, rather than discover 15-20 years down the road, during scandal, that positive values were never present (e.g., Enron, Fox News). We can learn from highly reliable organizations (e.g., aircraft carriers, nuclear power plants) that are obsessed with potential failure modes, and incorporate ways to recognize and avoid them.

In Phase 2, Discover Effectiveness, your team will search for effectiveness through a process of experimentation and validation, closely observing responses to its offerings in the real world. It is possible that no one has tested what it will take to achieve effectiveness in your situation. This book can tell you what it looks like, and can provide a process to find out, but until you observe effectiveness taking place (and verify that your efforts have induced it) you cannot be confident. The technique relies on the direct observation of demand-side behaviors in response to your offerings (i.e., products & services, or projects & programs). In predicting expected external behaviors, consideration of financial and economic benefit exchanges will be of interest, as well as social, psychological, spiritual, and environmental benefits. When your experiments discover what gets potential users excited and involved in your offerings, then you are unearthing the secrets...and you are discovering effectiveness. This book provides a way to think about what's involved, and lets you know when you have found a solution.

Management by Positive Organizational Effectiveness (M+OE) departs from the goal model, which has remained dominant in the daily practice of management around the world, but with limited success. Many people are familiar with Management by Objectives, which is based on the goal model. The goal model serves an aging, and largely top-down, bureaucratic reality. Let's call it "last century" technology. It is not reliable, because it accepts arbitrary goals that often focus on the wrong things. It leads to 'efficiencyism,' which marks the current age. As we will see, dysfunction is an emergent phenomenon under efficiencyism.

M+OE uses a new model, called the Outcome-focused Model (OFM) for organizational effectiveness. Within the OFM, the goal of every organization is the same, that is, to be effective within its environment. But effectiveness does not operate in the OFM at the level of the organization as a whole; it operates just below that, at the level of its individual offerings to the environment. Efforts to improve organizational effectiveness focus on an organization's *portfolio* of offerings that serve its environment.

Become Truly Great (the book) introduces an overriding directive: serve your environment & be rewarded in return.

To be truly great, you must first serve others effectively. You may have encountered a similar admonition elsewhere (e.g., Matthew 23:11, "the greatest among you must be your servant"). Serving your environment should not be considered casually, however, because evolutionary and adaptive pressures within the environment marginalize or cull organizations that are ineffective in serving it.

In Phase 1 (Be Virtuous), your organization examines its values to embed and retain the positive values necessary to achieve and sustain future greatness. In Phase 2 (Discover Effectiveness), your organization defines and tests the results chains associated with each of its offerings to calibrate and gauge their effectiveness. By the end of this phase, you will have come far, and your environment will be rewarding you already. In Phase 3 (Become Truly Great), your organization will need to be consistently effective for at least 5 years, working to improve the processes (and retain the values) that have been cultivated thus far. The final push toward true greatness is a cumulative process which aims to achieve positive and wide-spread impacts through continued effectiveness over time. It is about occupying (in a biological sense) one or more niches in your environment, because a great organization is integral (if not indispensable) to its environment, and acts to consistently build up (rather than tear down) the whole. Being great is not about 'winning,' which implies that someone else is 'losing.' Rather, it is about being recognized and rewarded by the environment for your service to it. "Serve your environment & be rewarded in return." It's a mantra for a new age, that is, The Age of Organizational Effectiveness.

ACRONYMS & KEY TERMS

AI – artificial intelligence

AGI – artificial general intelligence

AMJ – The Academy of Management Journal

CAS – complex adaptive systems

CDMA – code division multiple access (originally a radio spread-spectrum technology, now updated for cellphones)

CEO – chief executive officer

CRM – customer relationship management

C-Suite – refers to the executive suite of an organization, where titles begin with C (e.g., Chief Executive Officer, Chief Financial Officer, Chief Operations Officer)

CSR – corporate social responsibility

EEOs – expected external outcomes, or demand-side behaviors that verify the effectiveness of a designated results chain associated with an organization's products/services (or projects/programs)

Environment – an organization's environment is everything external to the organization — where customers, non-customers, other organizations, the economy, the natural world, and the rest of the universe are found.

EPA – US Environmental Protection Agency

GE – General Electric Corporation

IDWSSD – UN International Drinking Water Supply and Sanitation Decade (1981-1990)

IBM – International Business Machines Corporation

IBRD - International Bank for Reconstruction and Development (of the World Bank Group)

IDA – International Development Association (of the World Bank Group)

IFC – International Finance Corporation (of the World Bank Group)

IT – Information technology (the use of networked computers to process & display information)

ISIL – Islamic State of Iraq and the Levant

KPI – key performance indicator

LFA – Logical framework approach (includes participatory design with the beneficiaries)

Logframe – the logical framework (of RBM)

M+OE – Management by Positive Organizational Effectiveness

MIGA – Multilateral Investment Guarantee Agency (of the World Bank Group)

OE – organizational effectiveness

Offering – an organization's products & services (and/or projects & programs) being used to serve its environment

OFM – outcome-focused model, a new model (developed by the author) to define the concept of organizational effectiveness – using EEOs as the objective referent

POS – positive organizational scholarship

RBM – results-based management

ROI – return on investment

SMART (objectives or indicators) - $\underline{S}$pecific, $\underline{M}$easurable, $\underline{A}$ttainable, $\underline{R}$elevant, and $\underline{T}$imely

TQM – total quality management

UN – United Nations

UPS – United Parcel Service

US - United States of America

UNDP – United Nations Development Programme

VW- Volkswagen (German automaker)

WCDMA – wideband CDMA

WHO – World Health Organization

PART I

THE PRESENT AGE OF 'EFFICIENCYISM'

Part I consists of the first four chapters of the book, and addresses the present age of 'efficiencyism.'

Chapter 1 describes how current management practices often embrace efficiencyism, whether intentionally or unintentionally. Regrettably, organizational dysfunction is an emergent phenomenon under efficiencyism, which holds organizations back from achieving their true potential.

Chapter 2 discusses how the visible hand of managerial capitalism has displaced the invisible hand of free market forces in our economy over the last 250 years. Organizations are given a mandate to manage capitalism for the common good.

Chapter 3 finds that the CEOs of today's large public corporations often act like robotic overlords, although the forces of artificial intelligence have yet to take over the world.

Chapter 4 explores organizations as complex adaptive systems. In this view, organizations are made up of a collection of individual agents that have separate identities and interests, and who often function separately in response to the numerous stimuli that are present. This explains why dysfunction is an emergent property under efficiencyism.

In summary, Part I of the book briefs us on the present age of efficiencyism, so that we can put it behind us.

CHAPTER 1

'EFFICIENCYISM' IS HOLDING ORGANIZATIONS BACK

'Efficiencyism,' according to those that coined the term, is a belief in the tenets of efficiency without questioning its assumptions and consequences in specific circumstances (Schaefer and Wickert 2015). Of course, efficiency has a long-standing and largely valid tradition in management thought, and many of the early ideas about management revolved around efficiency. We could go back to Adam Smith's pin factory, where the specialization of labor allowed the pin factory to produce many more pins than could be produced if individual workers were carrying out all the steps themselves (Smith [1776] 2005, 11).

Early ideas about organizations envisaged a closed-system model where the organization had no need to interact with the external environment. This was useful in the early days because organizations (as we see from the pin factory) were trying to increase production through efficiency gains. It was assumed that the factory could sell whatever it could produce, because demand was high in the early days (the late 1700s and early 1800s).

As the industrial revolution matured, the new railroads in the USA introduced middle management, and larger organizations became possible using a bureaucratic model (i.e., more specialization of labor). As larger factories appeared, the economy was occasionally constrained by insufficient demand. Certainly, in recent decades, businesses cannot sell everything that they can produce. Factories are available that can produce many times over what the market can willingly absorb. The consumer is now in control.

It was Peter Drucker that reminded us of the four types of production processes known to man (Drucker 1973). The first is unique product production, which is what car companies used in their early days (late 1890's) when car parts were being made by hand in small factories, and it was the skill of the craftsman that determined how well the part fit. It was a slow, methodical, and difficult process — with little control, because workmen varied in their skills. Common processes often employed simple hand tools.

With the introduction of the assembly line, and more standardized production processes — Henry Ford's factories being some of the first (in 1913) — we see the second type of production, rigid mass production. Famously, when a Model T Ford came off the assembly line, the consumer could have any color he/she wanted, as long as it was black. That's the case with rigid mass production, everything must be the same. It is only with the introduction of flexible mass production (our third type of production process) that variation in sub-assemblies was introduced. For instance, a standard opening in the dashboard of a car (often found in the mid-1900s) allowed several different radios to be fitted into the slot. In the same way, different types of tires can be put on the wheels, because of the incorporation of standard bolt arrangements and standard tire sizes. Entire industries can then grow up to produce tires, to produce radios, or to produce many other things if the flexible mass production process is willing to accept these into the finished products.

The final type of production process is called process production, such as is found in refineries and certain kinds of steel mills. These run 24-hours a day for extended periods, and it is inefficient to shut them down or to start them up again. As we move from unique product production to rigid mass production and flexible mass production, we see great efficiency improvements. We also see the ability to customize the product (using flexible mass production) for the desires and demands of individual consumer groups. Even individual consumers can be accommodated when the order process is moved on-line (Internet) and the factory makes the product to specs. So, when we talk about efficiency, there is nothing wrong with pursuing efficiency in the mechanical sense of the word. And certainly, there have been many successes in organizations, as new technologies have brought improved efficiency over time. The difficulty comes when new technology interacts with the people in organizations, and results can be unpredictable. A few examples will be given shortly.

Despite the benefits of efficiency improvements, organizations need to move away from what has been called 'efficiencyism' — a sacred belief in the tenets of efficiency without questioning its assumptions and consequences. Efficiencyism, where and when practiced, can hold organizations back in significant ways due to its ability to bring about dysfunction. There are three reasons why efficiencyism holds organizations back: 1) systems theory tells us that an efficiency improvement in one part of an organization does not necessarily provide an improvement in the performance of the organization as a whole; 2) elevating efficiency to a sacred value (to be pursued at all costs) often leads to counterproductive actions at the first sign of financial trouble, such as layoffs, downsizing, and general efforts to do "more with less"; and 3) efficiencyism seldom works, because organizations are complex adaptive systems that can react in unpredictable ways when disturbed.

The first reason explains why information technology (IT) projects often do not produce the efficiency improvements that have been promised. An IT technology comes into an organization, usually addressing the efficiency of one or more of its processes. Even though it may increase efficiency locally, it does not necessarily improve the overall performance of the organization because the technology must interact with the people that are expected to use it, and those people must interact with other units in the organization — so that efficiency in one small part does not necessarily lead to overall efficiency improvements in the whole organization. In fact, organizational efficiency may be reduced overall. IT projects have failed for reasons of this type.

A few stories are offered here to describe the ways in which efficiencyism operates. It seems that dysfunction is a common emergent phenomenon in organizations that engage in efficiencyism, knowingly or unknowingly.

Sub-optimization. The efficiency of a company's parts can come at the expense of the efficiency of its whole. In their book *Reengineering the Corporation,* authors Michael Hammer and James Champy tell a story about a plane belonging to a major American airline that was grounded one afternoon for repairs at Airport A, but the nearest mechanic qualified to perform the repairs worked at Airport B. The manager at Airport B did not send the mechanic to Airport A that afternoon, however, because after completing the repairs the mechanic would have had to stay overnight at a hotel, and the hotel bill would come out of B's budget.

Instead, the mechanic was dispatched to Airport A early the following morning, which enabled him to fix the plane and return home the same day. In the meantime, of course, a multi-million-dollar aircraft sat idle, and the airline lost hundreds of thousands of dollars in revenue. Significant losses to the company occurred all because Manager B's budget couldn't allow for a $100 hotel bill. Manager B was neither foolish nor careless. He was doing exactly what he thought was right: controlling and minimizing the expenses of his unit (Hammer and Champy 1993) — a simple manifestation of efficiencyism.

Another example of sub-optimization occurred when the typewriter was introduced to people that were accustomed to writing by hand. The purpose of writing (let's say you are an author) is to get your thoughts down on paper and to organize them into a book. But if you didn't grow up using the typewriter, and you are present at the time that typewriters were first invented, you would have to learn how to type. We have all seen people using "hunt and peck" methods, where they use a single finger, to type something on the typewriter. So, even though the equipment has certain built-in efficiencies if you know how to use it properly, it can slow down the process (and reduce the overall efficiency) of getting thoughts on paper unless people and technology interact as expected.

A Shock to the Airline Industry. On the morning of September 11, 2001, I was at home in suburban Washington, D.C. Normally, I rode the Orange-Line Metro downtown to my office at the World Bank, but I was doing some work at home that day. When a UPS driver rang the doorbell to deliver a package, he seemed worried, and said that a plane had just crashed into one of the towers of the World Trade Center in New York City. I turned on the TV and soon saw a second plane crash into a second tower. It was 9:03 AM on the East Coast, and the United States was under attack.

In the aftermath of this well-known event that we call 9/11, the airline industry was reeling. Planes were grounded for three days throughout the country. Once they started to fly again, people were afraid to fly, and passenger traffic dropped precipitously. It wasn't clear that the domestic airline industry would survive. In the weeks following the event, many airlines laid off employees. Only Southwest Airlines and Alaska Airlines did not, among major US carriers.

James F. Parker, who had been CEO of Southwest for only a few months, faced some tough decisions in September 2001. "We just had to make a gut decision based on what we thought was important," he said (M. Glynn 2014). The decision was to give customers refunds if they wanted them, no strings attached. It was a risky policy for the company. If customers flooded the company with requests for refunds, the company could quickly exhaust the cash required to remain solvent. Fortunately, few customers requested a refund; instead, they generally opted for credit on future flights. Some even sent in small amounts of cash to the airline to show their support. Despite the uncertainty, Southwest went ahead and made a $179 million payment to the employee pension fund on time. Employees experienced no layoffs or reductions in pay.

In the three years after 9/11, researchers followed the performance of the 10 largest US airlines (Gittell, Cameron and Lim 2005). It was Southwest and Alaska that recovered most strongly and quickly, and those were the only two that had not resorted to layoffs. Before the event, they had the strongest cash reserves and the lowest debt, and engaged in a no-layoff policy. US Airways and United Airlines, who laid off 20-25% of employees and had high debt and relatively low cash positions prior to 9/11, recovered more slowly. Southwest Airlines was the only airline to show a profit in every quarter studied, while US Airways showed a loss in every corresponding quarter. No doubt, strong performance prior to 9/11 was important in building financial reserves, but so were decisions immediately afterward in terms of resisting employee layoffs. Crisis events lay bare the real values of a company and its management. In Southwest's case, grateful employees went out of their way to make the difference in company performance, while other airlines engaged in efficiencyism by imposing layoffs. This example highlights a destructive aspect of efficiencyism (i.e., the loss of social capital among employees following layoffs).

Ideologically-enforced austerity in government. The financial crisis of 2008 in the US hit the state of Michigan hard. An auto industry bailout undertaken by the federal government helped to avoid total collapse in the state, but local tax bases deteriorated state-wide due to a sagging economy. Debt became a significant issue in some communities that were already depressed. The Republican governor of Michigan (Rick Snyder) announced that the state would appoint emergency managers to reform the finances of any local government that was in a deep hole (Reed 2016). The overriding mandate was to get local budgets quickly under control. Flint, Michigan was one such case.

In 2013, Flint's emergency manager switched the water supply of the city from its existing but expensive source (Detroit city water) to a cheaper and close-at-hand source, the Flint River. As in many older communities in the US, lead pipes (some over a century old) made up a portion of the water mains in Flint. When the new water source (i.e., more corrosive water due to an absence of stabilizing treatment) flowed through the existing lead pipes, the water leached out small amounts of lead from the pipes and delivered it to the household taps. Residents began to complain about the discolored and foul smelling water almost immediately, but the emergency manager and the governor's office dismissed them as "anti-everything" critics, according to emails released (Reed 2016).

Before long, children in some households begin to show elevated lead levels in their blood. Children are most susceptible to lead poisoning because their brains are developing rapidly in the early years, and development disorders due to heavy metal exposure can be irreversible. Despite local complaints, state officials and emergency managers denied that there were problems right up until the time that a local pediatrician presented data about the high lead levels in children. When tests were run on water samples from the affected area, the EPA found lead levels that were, in some cases, 13,000 times the safe dosage (Reed 2016). It now appears that in trying to correct a financial problem, the governor's emergency manager had poisoned a large portion of the City of Flint, and had created a significant health emergency. In this example, efficiencyism displays its ability to lead politicians astray, despite several warning signs.

The hollowing out of IBM and other public companies. From the year 2000 to 2013, IBM pursued an aggressive strategy of share buy backs ($108 billion) and dividend returns to investors ($30 billion), while at the same time allocating comparatively little to capital investments ($59 billion). This was basically a financial engineering strategy that chased quarterly numbers, designed to adhere to IBM's so called Roadmap 2010, and later Roadmap 2015. The strategy proved to be exceptionally rewarding to CEO Sam Palmisano who managed investors' expectations and triumphantly engineered a soaring stock price before departing the company in 2012 with a $225 million severance package, including stock options, restricted stock, pension funds, and deferred compensation (S. Denning 2014).

Palmisano's supporters pointed out at the time that IBM's market capitalization had risen by $85 billion while he was CEO and that the company's share price gains had far outstripped those of the S&P 500 average. Detractors suggested that IBM was, thanks to its Roadmap 2010 & 2015, a ticking time bomb (Palmisano had gotten out while the going was good), and that his successor (Ginni Rometty) would have to deal with the wreckage (S. Denning 2014). The problem was the single-minded effort to grow earnings per share no matter the cost. CEO Rometty seems to be saddled with a need to continue the less-than-stellar mix of financial engineering tricks for the foreseeable future to grow earnings per share, despite the risks. In this example, efficiencyism leads a CEO to believe that creating shareholder value is an overriding directive, and that internal efficiencies should be pursued at all costs to attain it.

The Rise of "Downsize and Distribute." The machinations at IBM represent only the tip of the iceberg, however. Business leaders that present themselves as producers of prosperity in the economy can easily be the opposite (i.e., 'takers' rather than so called 'makers'). That is the point of an article entitled "Profits without prosperity" that appeared in the September 2014 issue of *Harvard Business Review* (Lazonick 2014). The author notes that the period after World War II until the late 1970s was characterized by a "retain-and-reinvest" approach to resource allocation in major U.S. corporations. Thus, they tended to retain earnings and reinvest them to increase the firms' capabilities. This served to benefit the employees who had helped make the firms more competitive and provided workers with higher incomes and greater job security.

The "retain-and-invest" pattern gave way in the late-1970s to a "downsize-and-distribute" regime where short term efficiencies were implemented involving layoffs, asset sales and other cost reduction approaches, followed by the distribution of freed-up cash to financial interests, particularly shareholders (Lazonick 2014). The downsize-and-distribute approach tends to strip value from a firm and contributes to employment instability and income inequality inside the firm because the firm's ability to be productive in the future has been weakened.

There seems to be more than one cause for the adoption of the downsize-and-distribute regime. Not insignificant has been the corporate raider model first employed by activists such as Carl Icahn, who employed asset stripping techniques in the 1985 hostile takeover of TWA. One example was that in 1991 he sold TWA's prized London routes to American Airlines for $445 million. Icahn later took TWA private and made a personal profit of $469 million while leaving TWA with debt of $540 million (Grant 2006).

Partly in response to these techniques, management of some publicly traded corporations have adopted counter-measures designed to make corporate raids and hostile takeovers less attractive, including legal poison pills, C-suite golden parachutes, and debt level increases on the balance sheet. Even after such measures, activist investors or hedge funds can buy as little as 10% of the stock of a public company to argue for a seat on the board and pressure management to increase returns to shareholders. Hedge funds have claimed that their efforts create a more efficient industrial structure and a better allocation of capital overall (ValueWalk staff 2015). It is doubtful, however, that history will be kind to the downsize-and-distribute regime, since it strips assets away and hampers a firm's ability to produce in the future.

Oversized Executive Compensation. Another trend during this period has been the widespread increase in executive compensation, largely influenced by the popularity of agency theory (championed by Milton Friedman and the Chicago School of Economics). Agency theory holds that C-suite executives are agents of the owners and need to be heavily incentivized to be sure that their interests are aligned with those of the owners (equated with shareholders). This has been a factor leading to generous compensation of the C-suite. Over the years, friendly boards have jacked up CEO compensation to extraordinary levels (tens of millions of dollars) by benchmarking with other firms that were doing the same (Whoriskey 2011). Starting with the 1980s, recent decades have seen a meteoric rise in executive compensation in the USA relative to the average worker's wage (Teather 2005). This is an example of the perverse incentives that operate under agency theory, and efficiencyism more broadly, due to misplaced and inappropriate objectives (i.e., shareholder value maximization).

The Downward Spiral at Sears. In 2008, Sears Holding Company CEO Eddie Lampert, previously a hedge fund manager and a big fan of Ayn Rand's objectivism philosophy, decided to bring dog-eat-dog competition into the firm (resulting from the merger of Sears and Kmart). He introduced a "warring divisions model" in which every executive would need to fight to win (Kimes 2013). Lampert divided the firm into dozens of autonomous groups that were to compete for attention and resources from the parent firm. When multiple executives are competing for what they need, however, overall company strategy takes a back seat to the needs of individual units. The problem that develops rather quickly is sub-optimization (E. Sherman 2015). Sub-optimization is a term that was used frequently in the 1990s when firms were trying to reengineer themselves into more efficient organizations. Not only were executives at war with each other, but cost cutting in recent years had reduced staff to the point where the customer experience was often unsatisfactory. Good luck, if you needed help from a salesperson in one of Sears' brick and mortar stores. As of February 2015, Sears Holdings had only one-quarter of the positive same-store sales that Sears and Kmart had separately before the merger (E. Sherman 2015).

What is efficiencyism? Efficiencyism holds up efficiency as a sacred value without the need for further examination, and the norm by which technological and social progress is judged. I use efficiencyism as something of a catchall term to characterize our current dysfunctional age (i.e., The Present Age of 'Efficiencyism,' described in Part I of this book). For me, efficiencyism encompasses a variety of memes in society that remain in the background, but which lead managers, consultants and C-suite executives to think and act in particular ways. In the above examples, it leads to layoffs, cutbacks, hollowing out of once great companies, and the old refrain about doing "more with less" at the first sign of financial difficulties. It can be seen among conservatives who want to "put government on a diet." Their view idolizes the free market, while contrasting "job killers" (bureaucrats and their government regulations) with job creators (businessmen who get things done). It urges decision makers to trust in free market capitalism, denigrate the role of government in our economy, and revere the role of business. Such thinking has gained traction in recent decades with the rise of a libertarian/ conservative narrative that has poisoned the public's mood toward government, and has attempted to elevate business and the free market to a point where they are seen to do little wrong. As we will learn, such views are flawed.

Efficiencyism can take many forms. The common thread has been the way that efficiencyism has worked its way into our psyche, and has led us into thinking in ways that are counterproductive. Efficiencyism typically emerges when C-suite executives and other managers try to make a single narrow objective into an overriding directive (whether it be maximization of profit, shareholder value, or anything else) and use it to justify efficiency improvements in parts of the organization. Such efforts may improve the efficiency of a part, but fail to improve the performance of the whole.

Efficiencyism is apparent when the goal model runs amok. Typically, unintended consequences appear somewhere in the organization. Dysfunction is an emergent phenomenon under efficiencyism, because organizations are complex (human) adaptive systems, and respond in unpredictable ways when disturbed. Now that you know what it is, and what to look for, you will probably find it everywhere. We must understand the fallacy of efficiencyism to move toward effectiveness.

CHAPTER 2

A MANDATE TO MANAGE CAPITALISM

The Invisible Hand, displaced by the Visible Hand

It has long been assumed that the invisible hand of the market provides unintended social benefits through individual (self-interested) actions, thus protecting and tempering capitalism and benefiting society. In this chapter, we will delve back to Adam Smith's world of the late-1700s to examine the mechanism of the invisible hand, then come all the way forward to Alfred D. Chandler Jr. and his 1977 book about the rise of the visible hand of management in society (A. D. Chandler 1977). In the end, I hope to show that the invisible hand, if it ever worked as claimed, was significantly diminished after 1840 when the railroads came on the scene in the United States. It was displaced by the visible hand of management, and that is where we remain largely today (except in parts of the economy where commodities prevail).

It has been said that Adam Smith was the first observer to describe the invisible hand. There is some debate in scholarly circles about that, as some of his contemporaries had similar ideas (Thornton 2009). Smith mentioned the invisible hand three times in his writings, but even then, it remains unclear whether he was referring to the market. In his classic book the *Wealth of Nations* there is only one mention of the invisible hand, and that relates to the support of domestic industry in relation to foreign industry. He said, "A merchant intends only his own gain, and he is in this and many other areas led by an invisible hand to promote an end which is no part of his intention. By pursuing his own interests, he frequently promotes that of society more effectively than when he really intends to promote it" (Smith [1776] 2005, 364). Today, there is a prominent view that the invisible hand of the market remains a dominant force in the economy. Conservatives, claiming alignment with Smith, typically argue that the market can be relied upon to regulate the economy and that government intervention is unnecessary and undesirable.

What was arguably true in 1776 when Smith's *Wealth of Nations* was published, may not be true today. We must remember that in those days' animal power was dominant upon the land and wind power upon the seas, so that production was limited, distribution was constrained due to the difficulties of travel, and most important, firms were very small. As late as 1840, and certainly prior to the 1770s when Adam Smith was writing, there were no middle managers in the United States. That is, there were no managers that supervised the work of other managers, and who then reported to senior executives (who were salaried managers themselves). Instead, enterprises were small (just a few people), so that the owners managed and the managers owned.

Alfred D. Chandler Jr., a well-known business historian, wrote that the visible hand of management has now replaced the invisible hand of the market (A. D. Chandler 1977, 1). He used several propositions to demonstrate how this happened gradually over time. For one, small traditional enterprise began to be replaced by multiunit enterprises when administrative processes permitted greater efficiency and higher profits than coordination by market mechanisms (A. D. Chandler 1977, 6).

As the US economy expanded, firms took advantage of growth opportunities by offering transactions under the control of the firm and taking them out of the market itself. This is a central point made in a paper by Ronald Coase (Coase 1937), for which he received the Nobel Prize in economics in 1991. Coase introduced the concept of transaction costs to explain why firms exist. For instance, if only market mechanisms were available, then customers would have to go to the market every time they wanted to conduct a transaction, whereupon they would incur information and negotiation costs as well as time costs, placing a restraint on what could be accomplished in a timely way.

Let me take you on a journey to illustrate the markets that existed in Adam Smith's time (in Scotland), and prior to the 1840s in the United States. When I joined the Peace Corps in the late 1960's, I was posted to Nepal. In Nepal, I was stationed at a village close to the center of the country at an elevation of about 4,500 feet. It was called Tansen (in the Palpa District), and I was a District Engineer for His Majesty's Government of Nepal. When I arrived, I found myself in an area that had no road, no running water, no electricity, and no telecommunications, so I was largely cut off from the rest of the world (unless I wanted to walk 18 miles to the nearest road, where I might find a bus). The local economy of Tansen had changed only marginally in the last hundred years.

In that economy (let's call it a free market economy), there were very small local shops, and traveling peddlers that would come by on a regular basis. I had to negotiate for everything. If I wanted to buy bananas in the morning (fresh picked that day), I would need to spend a few minutes with a traveling vendor haggling over a price (I could often get 6 or 7 bananas for one Nepalese Rupee – which was worth US$ 0.10 in those days). If I wanted to have a shirt made, I would have to go to a local cloth shop, sit with the merchant, and negotiate over the price of cloth (while also deciding how much I needed and of what type). Then I would take the cloth to the tailor, where we would discuss what it would cost to have a shirt made.

Everything was made on demand. It was unique-product production, in which an artisan, or specialist would make something specifically for the end-user. There was little standardization; quality varied, but depended upon the skill of the artisan. Some villagers bartered for goods in the market. A few mass-produced Indian goods were available locally, but you would have to go to India itself for uncommon items. Few consumer items were available. You were cut off unless you brought things with you. In summary, shopping in a truly free market necessitates a good bit of work (and cost) on the part of the consumer.

It wasn't until firms started incorporating transactions that would normally be handled by haggling in the market in earlier days, hiring staff to standardize and bureaucratize these transactions, that firms could grow significantly (early 1800s in the USA). By managing transactions internally, growing businesses saved costs by not having to use market mechanisms every time. Firm growth was also spurred by new technologies and the expanded markets that were emerging.

As a managerial hierarchy was being created and it was successfully carrying out its functions of administrative coordination, the hierarchy itself became a continuing source of power, permanence, and growth (A. D. Chandler 1977, 8). Later, we see the emergence of accountants and engineers, and other specialists of that sort as salaried managers became increasingly professional and technical. We also see the emergence of agents within the enterprise, separated from the owners, because as managers became more professional, the enterprise's ownership became distinctly separate from its management (A. D. Chandler 1977, 9).

The visible hand of management thus replaced Adam Smith's invisible hand of market forces where new technology and expanded markets permitted unprecedented growth in the volume and speed of material through improved production and distribution processes (A. D. Chandler 1977, 12). Before 1840, two or three men could administer the activities that any enterprise had regarding the distribution of goods; but after 1840, as the railroads expanded, and as steam power was harnessed in various industrial centers, production picked up significantly. As the USA moved beyond the 1840's, a different reality was emerging compared to Adam Smith's world, and managers of firms were taking a more active role in the economy. As they grew larger, firms simply incorporated transactions into their own orbit that had previously been carried out in the free market.

The coming of the telegraph in the late-1840's, together with the perfection of techniques first developed on the Western Railroad, helped to make travel by rail relatively safe, and it was the operational requirements of the railroads that demanded the creation of the administrative hierarchies in American business (i.e., middle management) (A. D. Chandler 1977, 87). The rail and telegraph companies were the first modern business enterprises to appear in the United States. They were the first to require many full-time managers to coordinate, control and evaluate the activities of their widely-scattered operating units. For this reason, they provided the most relevant administrative models for enterprises in the production and distribution of goods and services as those enterprises began to utilize the new transportation and communication networks.

This internalization of the activities and transactions previously carried out by many small units, well underway in the 1850's, was completed by the 1880's. The 1880's and the 1890's witnessed the culmination of technological as well as organizational innovation and standardization. In those years, the US railroads obtained a standard gauge and a standard time, and moved toward standard basic equipment in the form of automatic couplers, air brakes, block signals, and adopted uniform accounting practices. Thus, by about 1880, American railroad managers had taken on the appearance of a profession. They moved through life with a well-defined career path, and they had societies and journals that proclaimed their professionalism. By then they saw themselves (and were recognized by others) as a new and distinct business class, the first professional business managers in the USA (A. D. Chandler 1977, 132).

As enterprises grew to dominate significant portions of the economy they altered the basic structure of the whole (A. D. Chandler 1977, 10). Transactions within firms began to be dominated by institutionalized procurement processes that would have been very foreign to the world of Adam Smith. By the middle of the twentieth century, the salaried managers of a few large mass producing, mass retailing, and mass transporting enterprises, managed the flow of goods through the processes of production and distribution and allocated the resources to be used for future production and distribution in major sectors of the economy. By then, the managerial revolution in American business was complete.

The free market has been thought of as self-correcting, but transactions within firms are not cleared at free market prices. Rather, they remain slow and sticky, and less responsive to outside market forces because prices are now 'managed' by salaried managers. The idea that the visible hand of management has displaced the invisible hand of the market does not mean that market forces are irrelevant, but only that they take a back seat to the pricing freedom that firms enjoy for transactions captured internally.

The notion that the efforts of individuals to pursue profit through their own diverse interests benefits society more closely than if they had intended it from the start was an idea well suited to the small enterprises and free markets of the late 1700's, but does not ring as true today. Our economy is dominated by managerial capitalism rather than free-market capitalism. In the 250-years since Adam Smith's time, most transactions have been internalized within firms and are no longer carried out in the so-called 'free market.' Today, pricing is often 'managed' by a few giant firms in each sector, not due to collusion, necessarily, but simply due to their size dominance in the market. The self-correcting nature of market forces is often weak, except in commodity markets. The role of government in market regulation remains important.

This chapter has explored some of the forces at work in our economy. While firms have grown to encompass large chunks of the economy over the last 250 years, the visible hand of management has displaced the invisible hand of the market in significant portions of today's world. That should give us pause regarding the ability of markets to correct themselves, and to protect and temper capitalism in so doing. *The Economist* recently noted that as firms have grown to giant size, "the idea that market concentration is self-correcting is more questionable than it once was" (The Economist staff 2016b).

If our economy is dominated by managerial capitalism rather than free-market capitalism, then organizations are collectively managing the economy without fully realizing it. To improve their performance in this role, they need to incorporate a system of management that encourages organizational effectiveness, rather than problematic approaches to efficiency. In short, society's organizations (whether business, government, and nonprofit) need to enter the Age of Organizational Effectiveness so that they can, together, manage capitalism for the common good. Since today's managerial capitalism has largely displaced Adam Smith's free market capitalism, an organization is either part of the solution, or part of the problem.

CHAPTER 3

THE INTENTIONS OF THE ROBOTIC OVERLORDS AMONG US

One of the recurring themes expressed from time to time in the media is humanity's fascination, mixed with fear, that a humanoid robot equipped with artificial intelligence (AI) could be created, and that its kind would one day take over the world, perhaps subjugating humans in the process. This scenario is termed the "AI takeover." Some people have worried that as artificial intelligence progresses over time, this kind of horror is inevitable. Notable individuals such as Stephen Hawking, Elon Musk, and Bill Gates have called for research into measures that would keep AI under human control and thus make such an eventuality less likely (Sainato 2015).

Of course, intelligence in robots and in computers takes many forms, but the one that people most worry about is AGI, or artificial general intelligence, where computers act with the skill of humans. Some of the tests that have been used to distinguish whether AGI capabilities are present in a robot include common tasks that humans can do but robots have had difficulty in carrying out so far. One of them is the coffee test, in which a robot is sent into a typical American household and told to find the coffee machine, the coffee, the water, combine the ingredients, and push the right button to make the coffee. Another one is the college freshman test where the robot enrolls in college, attends classes, and takes exams just like a human would. There are other tests, of course, but I won't belabor the point here.

Factors that might make a future AGI takeover possible come down to basic biology and physics, coupled with consistent advances in computer technology. Our human brains are three pounds of tissue with a gelatin-like consistency, often termed 'wetware' rather than hardware. The brain houses our mind, and the mind is often thought of as the software of the brain. Though a human brain is a processing device, and is said to be the most complex object in the known universe, signals within the brain only move at about 100 miles per second, as opposed to a computer where signals move at the speed of light, which is 186,000 miles per second. In addition, biological neurons operate at a frequency of about 200 Hz, while the processing frequency of a modern computer has exceeded 2 Billion Hz. This means that computers have a significant, and growing edge in raw processing power over the human brain.

Aside from speculation about the eventual processing prowess of intelligent machines, the fear of robots comes down to a fear of their intentions, and particularly their goals and values. Our species seems obsessed with goals, some of which could be categorized as incredibly idiotic, harmful, and destructive. Goals can assume various forms, and can even become obsessions within the human mind, including the pursuit of money, fame, power, or any of a hundred other choices. There are several types of goals, that when pursued to the extreme, create bad results for humanity in general, although the individuals involved may feel fulfilled for a time. There is essentially no connection between how intelligent a being is and how appropriate its goals and values are. Any level of intelligence can be combined with any set of goals, including goals that are basically stupid and values that are immoral.

Least we spur panic among the population with such speculation, however, it is worth noting that neuroscientists are not as sanguine about the possibility of AGI, or as they call it, Strong AI. In their experience, the problem of Strong AI is much harder than is often assumed. A machine that could turn on us (or, alternately, truly love us) would need to have self-awareness, sentience, and consciousness, properties that are only found in humans. Thus, raw processing power alone is not enough to create a mind. That would require a being to have its own beliefs, desires, and motivations. In short, it would need to have intentionality and agency, and such qualities are unlikely to ever be found in robots (Azarian 2016).

Even if AGI does not emerge, there is no doubt that robotic processes could run off the rails if programmed with the wrong goals and values, coupled with sufficient power to achieve them. For instance, in a somewhat silly example, a robot that was a paperclip maximizer could theoretically destroy the world by continuing to produce paperclips at a rapid rate utilizing whatever inputs were handy. As we assign goals and values to robots and design processes for them to carry out, it would seem to be important to understand the implications to keep them from destroying us. Almost any goal, when taken to an extreme by a robotic machine that seeks goal maximization, may not turn out well.

That brings us to a discussion of the robotic overlords that are already here. Perhaps you have not recognized them as such. I am referring to the large computer / human integrations that are among us. This is where humans, generally operating in the belly of a large public corporation, pursue specific goals and utilize computer-driven processes to gain scale and speed advantages. The goals can take different forms. Whether it is the maximization of profit, shareholder value, or production, the single-minded pursuit of growth through goal maximization can be destructive in the long run. It is another manifestation of efficiencyism. Yet, there are self-reinforcing mechanisms in the stock market and elsewhere (including quarterly reporting for public companies) that perpetuate this unhealthy reality.

Companies that operate in robotic fashion often care little for their employees. One such employee described his experience in surviving a series of eight corporate layoffs in a hostile environment. When he became toast on the ninth, he said it was like being a prairie dog in a prairie dog town located next door to an angry farmer who occasionally leaned across the fence with a shotgun to take out a few of your fellow prairie dogs. You never knew when the next attack was coming. It wasn't until he had been laid off that he realized the amount of stress he had been living under.

Yes, robotic overlords are currently in place, and their goals and values are not congenial to most of us. *The Economist* has noted that the goal of shareholder value maximization (as reflected in the stock price) provides a license for bad conduct, including skimping on investment, exorbitant pay for the C-suite, high leverage in the financial makeup of the company, silly takeovers, accounting shenanigans, and large share buybacks — which have been running around $600 billion in the USA in recent times (The Economist staff 2016a). A corollary to shareholder value maximization is agency theory that holds that the Board and C-suite should be well compensated to align their interests with those of the owners.

Ironically, the short-term pursuit of shareholder value results in the destruction of shareholder value in the long run. It is not surprising that Steve Denning, writing in *Forbes* (S. Denning 2016b), has called this the second robber baron era, complete with the rise of monopoly power and little enforcement of antitrust regulations. Investment by public companies in their own businesses is running near historic lows, only about 4%, while profits are at record highs of 12% or so. We don't see the same problem in privately owned companies because different incentives are in place. There, investment is twice as high as in public companies. Main Street beats Wall Street in this area.

Peter Drucker noted in 1954 that the only valid purpose of an enterprise is to create a customer (Drucker [1954/1982] 1993). Some public companies listed on the stock market seem to have forgotten this truth. The current refrain from executives about "the stock market made us do it" is becoming a cliché somewhat akin to "the dog ate my homework." The reasons that we have robotic overlords in place is that shareholder value thinking coupled with agency theory has turned things back to front. Steve Denning believes that the root of the second robber baron era is essentially shareholder value maximization, which Jack Welch, the former CEO of GE has called "the dumbest idea in the world" (S. Denning 2016b). The problem is created by the single-minded pursuit of a goal in robotic fashion, particularly one focused on shareholder value maximization (providing another example of efficiencyism).

There is some history to what we see going on in large public corporations. The logic for shareholder maximization originated at the Chicago School of Economics with the support of Milton Friedman and his colleagues. His famous opinion piece in the *NY Times Magazine* (Friedman 1970) proclaimed (in response to the growing movement for Corporate Social Responsibility or CSR since the 1950s) that the sole social purpose of a firm was to make as much money as possible for its owners. The CEO was viewed as being ultimately responsible to the shareholders (equated with owners). Business schools and economics departments have been teaching shareholder value maximization ever since. But it is not true. Shareholders do not own the company; they only have a claim to some of the residual assets of the company via stock ownership. No-one owns a public company; it owns itself. As the British say, it's like the river Thames, nobody owns it (Kay 2015).

Even when conceding that shareholder value maximization should not be pursued due to an ownership argument, proponents still bring up a related argument for shareholder primacy (among all stakeholders). This too falls away, however, when the following is considered: 1) shareholders do not have the right of control over corporation assets; the Board of Directors has that right. Similarly, 2) shareholders do not have the right to help themselves to a firm's earnings; they only receive dividends when the Board of Directors sees fit. The claim that shareholders own the corporation is empirically incorrect from both a legal and an economic perspective (Stout 2002).

In this chapter, we have explored how the robotic pursuit of arbitrary goals (such as shareholder value maximization) can lead organizations astray. In coming chapters, we will explore a new approach that seeks to offer a better way forward — Management by Positive Organizational Effectiveness (M+OE). Within M+OE, the goal of every organization is the same, that is, to be effective within its environment. The effective organization understands its environment, serves it to the best of its ability, and is rewarded in return. It is not about single-minded pursuits such as the maximization of profit or shareholder value, but rather about creating products and services that offer real benefits to customers and elicit favorable customer behaviors. The demand-side always remains in control of whether any given benefit exchange will be completed. The supply-side cannot run full steam ahead unless the demand-side agrees. The achievement of effectiveness is a win-win-win for the organization, its customers, and its environment. Robotic overlords could not run amok if programmed to obey this production function. The future of the world may come down to simply programming the right goals and values into our robotic future. Of course, there is still the question of what we do about the robotic overlords that are currently in place.

CHAPTER 4

ORGANIZATIONS AS COMPLEX ADAPTIVE SYSTEMS

Examples in nature. What starts as a trickle can become a flood. With storm clouds overhead, I stand along a dry creek bed in Texas. As the rain starts, soon a trickle of water can be seen in the creek bed; it grows larger, and in time becomes a comparative flood. If I remain long enough, eventually the rain stops, and the creek bed goes back to its original dry state within a few hours. This is an example of a complex adaptive system. No one is in charge, yet the system self-organizes through the interaction of the drops of water with the land, and other features of the environment. A simple principle drives the system, that is, that water runs downhill to find its own level. The system undergoes a rapid phase transition, moving quickly from its static steady state where the creek bed is dry, to a dynamic state in which the creek is full of water. In most rainfall events, the creek bed provides a rigid constraint to contain the water and to channel it safely downstream;

but historic events can occur in which the supply of water overtops the banks and floods wide stretches of adjoining areas. As these events unfold, simple rules operate on the system to move it from a dry steady state, to wet turbulence, and back.

In the natural world, complex adaptive systems can be seen not only in stream beds, but in flocks of birds, schools of fish, and colonies of ants, among others. Within a flock of birds, individual birds synchronize their states in the flock based on simple local rules. No single individual controls the system, but order emerges from the interaction of individuals with others. In a school of fish, individual fish interact with each other in a nonlinear fashion, synchronizing their movements in rapidly changing patterns. In ant colonies, individual ants self-differentiate to conduct different tasks, although no one is in charge (including the queen). While there is no agreed definition of a complex system, emergent phenomena occur when complex systems function as an integrated whole, allowing consistent patterns to emerge from below.

Kodak. Trickles can become floods in other contexts, as well. Avi Dan, writing in *Forbes* (Dan 2012), noted that for 40 years you couldn't walk through Grand Central Station in New York without admiring the large 18 by 60 foot Kodak photographs displaying panoramas of America. They were designed to showcase the Kodak brand to travelers that passed through the station. In those days, Kodak marketing executives were adept at weaving the brand into the fabric of America, and they captured 90% of the US film market for generations. At the time, Kodak was one of the world's most valuable brands. But Kodak's story is ultimately one of failure, rooted in decades of success. Kodak didn't miss the digital age, rather, it invented one of the first crude digital cameras in 1975. Instead of fully developing and marketing the new technology in response to customer needs, however, the company held back so as not to hurt its lucrative film business (another example of inappropriate objectives under efficiencyism). By the 1990s, digital camera manufacturers found commercial success and began to disrupt the film market with their cameras.

What started as a trickle, became a flood. Kodak's profit peaked at $2.5 billion in 1999, but its share price decline precipitously after the year 2000 as the quality of digital photography was comparable to film and smartphones replaced cameras (The Economist staff 2012). In this new regime, only a small percentage of digital images were printed on Kodak film. Kodak declared bankruptcy in 2012, while its much smaller rival Fujifilm had a successful (but painful) rebirth through diversification, and continues to do well (Komori 2015). Kodak was culled by its environment because it did not adapt quickly enough to give customers what they wanted within the new and dynamic digital reality.

A valuable perspective. This chapter explores organizations as complex adaptive systems (or CAS). It is a valuable perspective for examining organizational performance because it reveals hidden patterns that can be found beneath the surface. In the past, such patterns did not lend themselves to study due to a lack of tools to examine what was going on. In the CAS perspective, organizations (and their environment) compose complex adaptive systems made up of individuals that can act on their own. These individuals are called agents, and typically include an organization's management and employees (internal agents), and their customers and other stakeholders (external agents). In such a system, despite efforts at top-down management, order often emerges from below based on the interaction of the agents with each other, producing observable phenomena such as an organization's "culture," a general sense of "how we do things around here," and customer demand.

Organizations are often thought of as conventional entities that are focused on specific goals and organized somewhat like a factory to achieve them. When the organization is threatened, it is anticipated that staff will react with one accord to counter the threat. But this model does not work reliably, especially when the environment in which an organization lives is changing rapidly. It would be useful if its members could react quickly like a flock of birds, each following its wingman in a coordinated turn. Humans don't seem to be able to execute this maneuver easily.

During periods of rapid phase transition, individuals, and social grouping within the organization can enter a state of uncertainty. Complex adaptive systems react in unpredictable ways at these times. When the system is far from equilibrium, individual employees may adapt to the new reality by either cooperating to fix the problem or, alternatively, display a non-cooperative or competitive attitude by rejecting the storyline that management offers. During transition periods, so-called 'attractor' regimes can emerge. For example, when confronted with a zero-sum game, such as outsourcing some jobs overseas, employees seldom cooperate. On the other hand, the positive-sum game presented by the expansion of a firm into a new segment of the market readily gains employee acceptance.

The complexity theory of organizations rejects the metaphor of organizations as well-oiled machines made up of replaceable parts. Instead, an organization's collection of internal agents has been brought together for a specific period, where they exhibit aspects of self-organization, emergence, and interdependency. Over time, the organization attempts to retain agents based on their individual contributions to the whole. Exemplary individuals are promoted while those that seem to be a poor fit are encouraged to go elsewhere. While these can be thought of as common

HR processes, it is important that a climate of fairness and good will be maintained throughout to avoid adverse behavior by those negatively affected. Efforts at performance measurement involving incentive-based pay, often thwart teamwork and overall organizational performance by enticing individuals to dance to their local incentives rather than taking direction from the larger organizational narrative. W. Edwards Deming, in his book "Out of the Crisis" (Deming 1982), was one of the first to point out the problems created by performance measurement in its various forms. In short, individuals are incentivized to game the system, while teamwork is hampered, internal competition is increased, and the performance of the organization itself suffers.

Adaptive pressures and evolutionary processes. On the macro level, organizations are part of their environment. Here they act as agents themselves on a larger stage, interacting with other organizations that frequent the same space. Within the macro environment in which organizations live, adaptive pressures and evolutionary processes are continuously acting. Individual organizations survive and thrive based on their ability to exchange benefits with their external environment through their offerings (see Chapter 7). When far from equilibrium and undergoing rapid change, the environment encourages an organization to adapt its offerings to remain relevant to the changing needs. In these situations, it can be important for an organization to have new offerings (of requisite variety) in the pipeline, ready for deployment. In a real sense, the environment selects individual organizations for retention based upon their effectiveness in serving its needs. On an aggregate and macro scale in individual sectors, evolutionary processes enforce "survival of the effective."

An example of adaptive pressures on an individual organization is Qualcomm. In May 2016, Qualcomm's

CEO Steven Mollenkopf described the dynamic nature of the tech environment to *The Street*, "What people kind of forget in the tech industry is that you are [in a battle of] life or death" (Sozzi 2016). A company like Qualcomm either makes a successful technology transition when necessary, or is no longer around, because the industry moves very quickly. Qualcomm has had to pivot several times either to a different end market or a different core competency, often rather quickly. One example Mollenkopf provided was the transition to WCDMA (an efficient wireless technology) and smartphones from earlier non-CDMA wireless technology. Such transitions come along about every five years, he noted, but the company needs to make sure that it always hits the next transition very well (Sozzi 2016).

Finding their mojo. There are two extremes that organizations may experience, homeostasis and chaos. Homeostasis can be represented by an old-style bureaucratic organization in equilibrium, where the goal is predictability and stability. Chaos is the opposite state, where an organization is operating far from equilibrium and is in a state of turbulence, typically brought on by a catastrophic event. Neither of these extremes is conducive to effective performance. Between the two extremes, but just short of the onset of chaos, organizations can find their mojo. Here, random events in the environment can be amplified by feedback loops and open important new pathways toward the future. Here, Apple found the iPod, iPhone, and iPad to be effective; Google monetized search; Amazon has disrupted retail. Similarly, Southwest Airlines recovered rapidly from the shock of 9/11, as their employees rallied behind a common cause (Chapter 1).

Narratives as Attractors. Narratives can shape the way in which agents behave in an organizational system. Narratives are simply stories. Good stories can place an organization's goals and objectives in context, and explain how the organization expects to convert its skills and resources into offerings that are meaningful to its customers. Narratives have an ability to attract, and can become attractors within a complex adaptive system. A positive narrative can give employees a sense of purpose and the ability to connect their own behaviors with the larger goals of the organization itself. When employees feel that they are part of a larger purpose – helping not only their customers, but their fellowman in a larger sense – they have a greater social connection with each other, with society, and with their organization.

Attractors become important as we think of the approaching future, and how to guide the future into the present to take advantage of its most promising aspects. If you ride a train and look at the distant hills, you will see the hills approaching. Of course, the train is moving toward the hills, but the view would be the same if the hills themselves were approaching. This image is similar to how we should think about the future flowing toward us, and what we need to do to prepare ourselves — by investing in certain hard and soft resources that can serve to guide and determine which future emerges from the possibilities before us.

For instance, if you think of yourself as a young person looking toward college, and you imagine a future life — many futures are possible. You must prepare yourself for a desired future through your school work, however: going to school, taking relevant courses, and then emerging on the other side just as the future you had prepared for arrives. The skills that you gain, and the academic degree that you walk away with, serve as both constraints and attractors to shape your future possibilities.

In the same way, a company that invests in new equipment will make it possible to produce products at lower cost and higher efficiency, attracting and gaining in the process certain customers that would otherwise be unavailable. So, as the future comes toward us, narratives can serve as attractors that guide company actions in the present, and enable the enactment of futures that we have envisioned for ourselves.

In the national election of 2016 in the US, the voters faced a choice between the Democratic and Republican parties (as usual). The narratives of each of these parties (and their respective candidates) served as attractors to lead voters in the direction of one candidate or another for President. Narratives that we hear in the media, and that come to us through our televisions and radios (and across the Internet), are not subject to verification directly via first-hand knowledge. So, it is important that the validity of news sources be verified before buying into a narrative. A lot of false information circulated in the media during the election season, and new parts of the narrative appeared even in the final days. False narratives can lead us to vote for one or the other candidate for spurious reasons. Candidates that espouse false or misleading narratives can lead us in directions that may even be highly destructive. Despite the negative nature and questionable validity of some of the available information, political narratives clearly have extraordinary power to act as attractors to align voters' preferences with one candidate or another – a phenomenon that was on display during the final days of the 2016 election. Although the polls may not have been wrong leading up to the election (as each reflected the situation at a single point in time), it appears that a significant number of voters changed their election day strategy in the final days in a rapid, non-linear fashion, typical of behavior in complex adaptive systems. The result on election night was surprising, and disconcerting (i.e., the election of Donald Trump).

Within organizations, the overall narrative of the organization, including its goals and how it expects to achieve them, are typically put forth by official sources. The official version can be verified for authenticity through conversations with internal sources and by observation of behaviors that can be observed internally and externally. This means that organizational narratives are verifiable, based on triangulation with multiple internal and external sources. False narratives within the context of an organization can be detected through a conflict between sources, including the official narrative, the informal narratives that we hear from internal sources, and observation of behaviors around us. If all sources are in alignment with the official narrative, we can feel confident that it is being acted upon in a deliberate manner. However, when we find sources are not in agreement, or observed behaviors that do not ring true, we begin to question the direction that the organization is taking.

Internal actors can and will act on their own in the absence of narratives that align their actions with the official narrative, and with the internal truth. Dysfunction can be emergent under such conditions. Positive narratives can serve as attractors to align the behavior of internal agents with future states that the organization has envisaged for itself. For successful alignment, look for organizational narratives that reflect positive values, and that can be authentically voiced in a consistent way by internal and external sources.

This chapter has looked at organizations as complex adaptive systems (CAS). In this view, organizations are made up of a collection of individual agents that have separate identities and interests, and who often function separately in response to the numerous stimuli that are present. The CAS perspective provides a set of tools to look at organizations in new ways, and to understand what is going on. It offers a different view of the world. The CAS perspective deals with what has been called "the interesting in-between," far from equilibrium, but just short of chaos. Here, surprising phenomena can emerge from below as parts of the system interact as an integrated whole. It also explains why dysfunction is an emergent phenomenon under efficiencyism. While Kodak remained focused on its profit in film, consumers abandoned the brand for digital alternatives. Caution is advised with CAS — what starts as a trickle can become a flood.

PART II

THE COMING AGE OF
ORGANIZATIONAL EFFECTIVENESS

Part II of the book is made up of Chapters 5 - 11, which focus on topics that you will need to understand and take on-board before entering the Age of Organizational Effectiveness.

Chapter 5 describes how to examine your organization's values to see if they are sufficiently strong and virtuous to sustain you on the journey toward greatness.

Chapter 6 asks whether organizations are sufficiently meaningful. It considers how we arrived at the current situation, and how organizations can be more meaningful in the future.

Chapter 7 constructs a new synthesis of theory on organizational effectiveness that can help us depart the current morass of efficiencyism.

Chapters 8 - 10 consider new paradigms in management thought that have been proposed in recent years, specifically Steve Denning's "radical management" (Chapter 8), the shared value concept from Michael Porter (Chapter 9), and the purpose-driven organization (Chapter 10). We consider whether these new ways of thinking are ushering in a new age.

Chapter 11 suggests that for the world to be saved -- and many observers agree that it will be necessary in the future -- then it will require effective organizations to do the job.

In summary, Part II of the book takes us on a significant journey. In the end, it deposits us at the gate of the new age. It is preparing us to enter the Age of Organizational Effectiveness in Part III of the book.

CHAPTER 5

BE VIRTUOUS (PHASE 1 OF M+OE)

Being intentional about being virtuous. As I was writing this book, the working title changed frequently. In the beginning, it was largely about how organizations can become effective, since that was the initial problem I wanted to solve. Although I was aware of it from the start, it took a while to internalize the fact that bad actors can be effective, and that I needed to address the problem in the book. There have also been examples of organizations in the past that have appeared to be effective for a time, but eventually came to grief because of rot within. It seems that organizations are often unprepared to hold internal agents accountable to a common set of positive values until it is too late. To be virtuous, organizations need to be intentional about it. That's why 'Be Virtuous' (the title of this chapter) represents Phase I of Management by Positive Organizational Effectiveness (M+OE).

Straying to the dark side. Examples are numerous of organizations that have strayed to the dark side by embodying negative values in various forms — including Enron, WorldCom, Volkswagen, the World Football Federation (FIFA), Toshiba, and Bernard Madoff Investment Securities LLC. Several organizations have appeared to be paragons of performance, riding high before scandal, and whose names seemed to be synonymous with some form of greatness; but these same organizations were brought low by one or more people within the organization that behaved in non-virtuous ways.

In the case of Enron, management used off-balance-sheet accounting tricks and complicated financial instruments that intentionally hid the truth from investors. Eventually it was found that the real value of the company was considerably lower than the stated book value, causing a precipitous loss in the stock price, and bankruptcy in 2001 (Oppel and Sorkin 2001).

In 2015, Volkswagen (VW) was trying to take over leadership in the auto industry and was selling a lot of diesel vehicles worldwide. At the height of this apparent success (despite the self-serving goal), a scandal emerged by chance. A small lab at the University of West Virginia started testing diesel engine emissions on the road to understand how VW diesels were able to achieve their high mileage ratings. The new tests were conducted on the open road, as opposed to the test bed where the vehicles had been certified in conformance with standards. It turned out that because of deceptive software within their engine monitoring system, VW diesels were producing emissions on the road that far exceeded standards in the USA (Glinton 2015). The lab's findings created a major scandal at VW, and a great brand was significantly tarnished.

In another example, Bernard Madoff was well-known in the securities industry and was believed to be an upstanding leader (as a former chairman of the NASDAQ stock market). Eventually it was discovered, however, that his investment firm was simply a Ponzi scheme, and that over $50 billion worth of hidden fraud had gone undetected (The Economist staff 2008).

If we choose to expand our search to the shadowy and violent side of organizational performance, we could find somewhat effective but negative examples among drug cartels, and even terrorist organizations like ISIL or al Qaeda. Organizations such as these are likely to have relatively short and precarious trajectories, as state actors in the environment are mobilized and coordinated in efforts to eliminate them.

Why be virtuous? Virtuousness should be considered as a prerequisite for greatness. Virtuousness in organizations is about instilling positive values and being sure that those values consistently result in positive behaviors within the organization. An organization needs to live its values and love its purpose. While values may change over time, they express beliefs and attitudes that permeate the organization, and help shape its culture. Values can also include attributes that the organization wants to maintain at a high level of reliability and resilience.

Traditional business values have included things like efficiency, profitability, and management control, but these need to be balanced against higher values and virtues to help the organization aspire to greatness and connect its values to the common good. Here we see a need for management to lead the way. It is often the leader of the organization that embodies the values and acts as an example to others on how to live those values within the organization. An example of positive values, together with organizational virtuousness, would be the US Marine Corps — for the way it instills values within its members.

A useful parallel on how to instill virtuousness in organizations is illustrated by the methods used in high reliability organizations, such as aircraft carriers, nuclear-powered stations, air traffic control, and forest firefighting. These situations are dangerous and prone to error, and errors that are experienced can be devastating and costly. High reliability organizations are quite sensitive to, and preoccupied with, failure. They have identified the main modes of failure, and have implemented safeguards and checks to be sure that they do not occur. Such organizations contain a high degree of expertise, and work hard to keep their operations stable and failsafe. Using a similar approach, positive virtues and attributes can be intentionally instilled in an organization to amplify performance and to protect it from specific failure modes.

A good example of organizational virtuousness was the cleanup work conducted at the Rocky Flats nuclear waste site (Colorado), where there had been a long history of nuclear weapons production. When an estimate was done of how much it would cost and how long it would take to clean up Rocky Flats, the estimate was for 70-years and $36 billion dollars. What makes this an amazing story, however, is that the work was completed 60-years early, while saving almost $30 billion in taxpayer funds due to the positive values and outstanding work of the clean-up contractor, Kaiser-Hill (Hess and Cameron (Eds.) 2006). The remediated nuclear waste site is now part of a wildlife refuge.

Phase 1 of M+OE is 'Be Virtuous.' In Management by Positive Organizational Effectiveness it is important to start from a position of virtuousness in an organization, then discover effectiveness to become great. It is the values and virtues which are inculcated in the personnel carrying out the processes that set the organization up properly to eventually become truly great. If the intention is to become truly great, it would be difficult to argue that an organization should not clothe itself with virtuousness before starting the journey. The founder of Patagonia, Yvon

Chouinard, noted in a recent interview that the values his company began with were critical in charting the course of its later success. Google, in its original outline of mission and vision talked about "don't be evil." Alphabet, which is the successor to Google, now calls for "doing the right thing" but Google still mentions "don't be evil" within its admonitions to employees. It is the adherence to positive values and virtues that amplifies performance and protects the organization from falling into a ditch along the path to greatness. To be more intentional about its values, an organization needs to take the viewpoint of an outside observer and make an honest assessment of what values are expressed within its processes and culture.

Taking your values to the bank. Let's take a moment to look at the issue of virtuousness from a practical perspective. It is all well and good to have virtuous values, but what good are they? Can an organization take its values to the bank? Well, yes it can. Let me explain.

There are three important reasons that an organization needs to be intentional about its values, virtues, and attributes. The first reason is because they *amplify* the demand-side responses to the organization. We all want to interact with virtuous organizations. Virtuousness, if it is fully enacted and can be relied upon by customers as part of an organization's DNA, can be a competitive advantage. It comes into play when we talk about effectiveness. For instance, effectiveness is about converting the supply-side intentions of an organization into the demand-side behaviors of uptake, adoption or use (as we will see in Chapter 7). When demand-side actors can believe in the virtuous attributes of the organization, that knowledge becomes compelling in terms of a narrative to attract engagement – thus amplifying the benefits that are exchanged between the organization and its customers.

Let me give an example. I was recently in a McDonald's Restaurant, and I was given a brochure that outlined the (new) food philosophy of McDonald's (i.e., The Simpler the Better™). "We've heard you," it said. "As a restaurant, we're proud to say we've made some changes for you, our customers, because where would we be if it weren't for everyone who walks through our doors daily?" The brochure provided a list of things that had been changed. For example, it noted that McDonald's Expresso beans are now sustainably sourced from the Rainforest Alliance Certified™ suppliers. On chicken, "we serve chicken that has not been treated with antibiotics important to human medicine." On fish, "we only use wild-caught Alaskan Pollock from sustainable fisheries in our Filet-O-Fish, and we've never stopped being inspired by sustainable practices like these to embrace new ones."

The basic point I want to make is that McDonald's has expressed some (updated) values in the handout. It's an attempt to change the narrative that runs in our heads as we decide where we want to eat. If I am a member of the millennial generation, I might believe in sustainable practices for my coffee, and not in antibiotics in my chicken. I'm not going to pull into the parking lot if I know that McDonald's doesn't care about these things. So, an organization's values are acted out in the specific attributes that are attached to its offerings. These attributes become either attractors or detractors in efforts to engage customers, and help them to quickly decide whether they want to accept the products and services being offered.

If the attributes that are being offered are not those that I prefer, then I'm likely to go somewhere else. So, when an organization includes values in its narrative, it is taking them to the bank, because a portion of the subsequent transactions wouldn't occur unless the values were present, they were expressed, and they were guaranteed. Values, expressed as attributes in products become go or no-go decisions for the customer. If you have products with the preferred attributes, then they are going to buy from you. You can take that to the bank. In short, expressed values become amplifiers that help attract consumers to your products.

The second reason to be intentional about values is because of the *diversified workforce* that is becoming common in many organizations, as more people with diverse backgrounds enter the workforce. Today's workers are different in several respects from earlier generations – more women, minorities, people from different national origins, diverse backgrounds, and young and older workers mixed together. In any organization, but especially within this melting pot, it is unknown what values may be dominant. If left unattended, we can expect a culture to emerge from the bottom through the interaction of individuals over time, as it would in any complex adaptive system. It is important that the organization itself be intentional about what values it wants in the workplace, however, by identifying those values, incorporating and guaranteeing them in its processes, and self-monitoring them over time. These should include positive values such as openness, honesty, decency, doing what's right for the customer, and other values that may be important depending upon the individual situation within each organization.

The third reason to be intentional about values is because positive values are *protective.* Values embedded within processes and culture can protect an organization from problems along its journey. For instance, Wells Fargo was recently in the news because some 5,000 employees created bogus credit cards for customers without their permission and we're reaping some incentive rewards internally. Would that have occurred if the internal pressures had been different? What about the culture? Could it have been protective, but was not?

And what about Fox News? CEO Roger Ailes of Fox made his own news in 2016 when a sexual harassment suit was brought against him. Fox paid a single $20 million settlement to Gretchen Carlson, and perhaps others that came forward to accuse Ailes. Fox's values are suspect because of what has gone on there, including "grotesque abuses of power…a culture of misogyny, and one of corruption and surveillance, smear campaigns and hush money" (G. Sherman 2016). What if other values, more positive values, had been in place? Would they have been protective? And what of the culture that has supported a corrosive environment for the last 20 years, with implications far beyond the man at the top? Based on available reports, Mr. Ailes appeared to be very intentional about the values in place at Fox News; unfortunately, they were negative values.

This chapter has explained the reason for the 'positive' emphasis in Management by Positive Organizational Effectiveness, and why 'Be Virtuous' is Phase 1 of M+OE. It has also provided a few ideas about how positive values can be of great benefit to an organization (or negative values can create great harm). Positive values can serve to amplify benefit exchanges with the environment, orient a diversified workforce to what the organization considers important, and serve as a protective shield against scandal over time. They can become differentiators that define and distinguish your brand. Once in place, be sure to inform your customers what values and attributes you bring to your offerings, and why you consider them to be important. This is what McDonald's was attempting with their brochure.

CHAPTER 6

MEANINGFUL ORGANIZATIONS

Shouldn't organizations be meaningful?

The theme of the Academy of Management's annual meeting in 2016 was 'Making Organizations Meaningful.' Within the promotional literature for the conference, the Academy noted that "organizations occupy a central role in the way that we live our lives, for better or for worse. They enable us to be more efficient, to access goods and services faster than ever before, to share information and experiences around the globe, and yet organizations are not unproblematic. There have been highly publicized scandals, Wall Street corruption, failure of government to meet the needs of its citizens, and public distrust and questioning of organizations and their reasons for being. It is often taken for granted that an organization's purpose is to produce economic value, and although economic value can often add to social value, sometimes it does not. This disjunction raises the question of meaningfulness. Meaningfulness of an organization is its expression of purpose, values, or worth, and it involves a sense of significance that goes beyond material success or profitability. It highlights how organizations can play a larger and more positive role in the world" (M. A. Glynn 2016).

The next generation of workers, the millennials, are searching for meaning in their work, not simply a paycheck. They want to make a positive difference in the world through their contribution to society — in organizations, not despite them. They want to know *why* they should do something, not just *what* to do. "…'Just because' isn't going to work for me," says Liz (age thirty), in Lee Caraher's book, *Millennials & Management* (Caraher 2015).

How did we lose meaning?

Going back to the Greeks and the Romans, if not before, writers and poets extoled the virtues of the farmer and herdsman in song and in poetry. Artisans were the main producers of consumer goods prior to the Industrial Revolution. The European tradition was for artisans to pass on their knowledge to an apprentice (often from the same family) who learned the trade over a lengthy apprenticeship. It was taken for granted that artisans derived a good deal of meaning in their work, and had an established place of honor in their village or community. The butcher, the brewer, and the baker that Adam Smith referred to in his book *Wealth of Nations* (Smith [1776] 2005, 19) would have been considered local artisans.

Now, a few hundred years later, capitalism is at a crossroads. It has something of a bad name. Blue collar workers have seen their wages stagnate, and worse, many jobs have been outsourced to lower wage countries. When on the job, workers often seem disengaged from their work, and may derive little meaning from it. Many white collar contingent workers live in the 'gig economy.' In the USA, we find an economy with low growth, and workers who feel that their jobs are at risk. Full-wage pay with benefits has become more difficult to find and retain. Whereas in the past, companies tended to invest in workers and retain them throughout their career, now it is common for organizations to simply shed workers during downturns when they are not required. This shifts the employment risk from organizations to workers. The election of Donald Trump, the Republican candidate in the 2016 US Presidential Election, brought voters' anxiety in this area into sharp focus.

One of the first questions is, "How did we get here?" I would argue that it's been a path-dependent journey. We are where we are because of events that have led us to this moment. Other paths could have been taken; the future is also path dependent, and collectively we must chart the course. Let's take a quick trip through history, to learn from it.

I would start with Adam Smith and the pin factory that he described in his book *Wealth of Nations* (Smith [1776] 2005, 11). The pin factory illustrated specialization of labor, or breaking up the tasks within the factory so that each worker carried out a small but specific step in the process. Thus, the factory could produce many more pins after the specialization of labor than was the case before. At an earlier time, with individual workers doing all the tasks necessary to make a product, it was a slow and laborious process. So, back in Adam Smith's day supply was constrained by the inefficiencies of the production process. The only problem with specialization of labor (e.g., in a pin factory) was that it often created mind-numbing boredom for the worker. Is this the beginning of today's lack of meaning in work?

In Adam Smith's day, factories could not produce goods efficiently because owners and managers had little understanding of production methods. The Industrial Revolution was still in an early stage, and many improvements were to come. In those early days (before 1800), firms were very small; owners managed and managers owned, and free market capitalism prevailed. Transactions were being carried out in the market, where haggling took place between buyers and sellers. As we progressed into the 1800's and up to the 1840's (when railroads began to appear in the US), middle management began to appear (A. D. Chandler 1977).

Bureaucracy was an innovation of the mid-1800s. It provided for specialization of administrative functions into various departments (more specialization of labor). Transactions were gradually brought inside firms, where they were conducted according to routine processes, with standardized ways of doing things. Gradually, this took transactions out of the free market, creating what Alfred Chandler calls managerial capitalism (A. D. Chandler 1977). As firms grew, more transactions were incorporated into firms, and the managerial economy grew further. By the latter part of the 1800's, firms had grown to large size through vertical and horizontal integration, ushering in what writer Mark Twain termed the Gilded Age. Much of the growth in the US had been due to the expansion of the railroads and the telegraph, together with the firms that could utilize railroad transport to distribute goods to far flung cities from factories in the Northeast.

In 1911, Frederick Winslow Taylor published *Scientific Management*, which was about improving the efficiency of men at work (Taylor [1911] 1998). Taylor had sought to establish the "one best way" for each task, to show the workers how to do their work in the most efficient way possible. As incentive, his methods had the advantage of increasing the wages for those men that were willing to take direction from Taylor-like managers, and, for the owners, efficiency was increased in firms that took up Taylor's methods.

By the 1940s and WWII, the great need for war material from the USA necessitated the ramp-up of production through the wide-spread use of training methods for workers (largely women). Then, in the post-war period of the 1950s and 1960s, much of the world had to be rebuilt, and that time is remembered fondly as a golden age in which American-made products did very well around the world. By the seventies, however, oil price shocks from OPEC arrived, together with significant inflation. By the 1980s, Reaganomics identified big government as the problem rather than a source of solutions. The personal computer was invented in the early eighties, and by the end of that decade, use of the personal computer had grown considerably in business. The 1990s saw the emergence of the Internet, and we are still at an early stage of follow-on effects that derive from that event. In the 00's, we had the 9/11 attack, a couple of wars, and today the pall of terrorism continues in various forms.

We have come to the present, where demand remains quite low in historical terms for most goods and services. Today's factories can produce several times over what today's consumers seem willing and able to buy. The economy is experiencing slow growth, wages are modest, and workers are at risk. During the period 1950-1980, the compensation of hourly workers improved in step with gains in productivity; after 1980, however, hourly workers' wages stagnated and much of the subsequent gains in productivity were retained by organizations and their shareholders (S. Denning 2016a). Much of the risk that companies earlier assumed in hiring workers has been laid at the feet of the workers themselves. The jobs of blue-collar workers are at risk because automation in high-tech factories at home and abroad has reduced the need for manual workers. White collar contingent workers are also at risk because the "gig economy" is becoming the new norm. There is a popular view that trade deals with other countries have resulted in the export of good jobs from the USA to other countries in recent decades in search of lower wages.

The sweep of history has moved us away from an economy constrained by supply (in Adam Smith's time), when factories were small and inefficient. Sometime around the 1930s, and then into the 1970s-1990s and beyond, the US economy became constrained by demand. We are still in that mode in the US, and increasingly around the world, although there have been growth spurts along the way. The consumer is now sovereign. Over time, as outlined in the above discussion, the drive for economic efficiency has introduced forces and tensions that now challenge the sense of meaning that we find in our work, our organizations, and in our lives.

The path forward

Where do we go from here? Can organizations provide meaning to work in a predictable way? The old model was one of command-and-control. Management was in control, they set the objectives, and employees answered to the C-suite for their achievement. During the "retain and invest" regime mentioned earlier, this was not a significant problem. Workers were relatively happy at the time, because they felt the organization was keeping their interests in mind.

Now that "downsize and distribute" is common, however, stresses have built up around the social contract between management and workers. In the 1980's, C-suites began to receive incentives to improve shareholder value (and heighten their own self-interest). This trend emerged as part of a drive by conservative business schools to champion agency theory, wherein manager-agents were aligned with owners (equated with shareholders) through the provision of stock options to improve performance. CEO compensation began to increase rapidly in public companies as a result. Corporate mergers and hostile takeovers also became prevalent, based on attempts by activist investors to unlock shareholder value from existing firms. Hedge funds began making a case for shareholder value in annual board meetings, stating that shareholders should be given priority above other stakeholders. The logic of agency theory and shareholder value maximization remains prevalent today, despite evident problems that have emerged with the approach.

If the old command-and-control model driven by C-suite objectives is no longer working, the new model must be something different. One aim of this book is to think through what that would look like. In coming chapters, we offer Management by Positive Organizational Effectiveness (M+OE). It is a new way to manage organizations, in which the goal of every organization is to be effective within its environment. It replaces the arbitrary objectives from the C-suite (such as profit or shareholder value) with an overriding directive to serve your environment & be rewarded in return.

Within M+OE, a meaningful path forward for management and workers involves the search for new and creative ways to serve the organization's external environment — home to customers, non-customers, and others with needs that the organization has ignored for too long. The environment offers opportunities to prosper, not simply by exchanging financial and economic benefits associated with product and service transactions, but by recognizing and pursuing other types of benefit exchanges (e.g., social, psychological, spiritual, and environmental). Non-profits are showing the way in these areas.

To take advantage of the opportunities within M+OE, an organization needs to derive understanding and meaning from the signals that are being given off by the environment, answering those signals with a portfolio of products and services that address the perceived needs. Dr. Otto Scharmer of MIT has noted that to transform business, organizations need to consider the co-creative power of stakeholder communities. Likewise, to transform government, organizations need to find new forms of direct and distributed democratic engagement (Scharmer 2015).

Overall, an important way to convey meaning is through the stories that organizations tell. As we saw in Chapter 4, a narrative can become an attractor that aligns individuals within the organization with the greater purpose to be served by joining in collective effort. It can give meaning to the organization's reason for existence and the overall value proposition being offered to its environment. Organizations create meaning for themselves and others by linking what they do to a larger narrative that benefits society (and the larger environment), thus merging internal and external views of the path forward, and providing a promising solution to organizational meaning going forward. The derivation of meaning from work is what organizations and workers have been searching for, and what they need for fulfillment. Truly great organizations will fulfill these needs.

CHAPTER 7

FINALLY,
A CONCEPT OF EFFECTIVENESS

This chapter offers a new synthesis of theory on organizational effectiveness to give the reader an understanding of the roots of our approach to management (i.e., Management by Positive Organizational Effectiveness) and the specifications of our concept of effectiveness. It was Kurt Lewin, the founding father of social psychology, who famously surmised that "there's nothing so practical as good theory" (Lewin 1951, 169). Good theory can turn knowledge into wisdom, and offer predictive value in the face of uncertainty.

To the layman, defining and determining the effectiveness of an organization may seem like a straightforward inquiry: to ask about effectiveness is to question how well an organization is doing with respect to some set of standards (Scott 1992, 318). While this view is not wrong, organizational scholars have found that the pursuit of this simple question leads one to complex and controversial issues, where numerous value judgments must be made, and no agreed standards are available to provide guidance. Among individual scholars, diverse conceptions of organizations can be found, and each of these conceptions offers distinctive criteria for evaluating organizational effectiveness (K. S. Cameron 1986). In addition, several constituencies will have an interest in questions surrounding the effectiveness of an organization and each is likely to propose criteria that support their interests (Pfeffer and Salancik 1978) (Hrebiniak 1978) (Zammuto 1984). What may start out as a straightforward inquiry can easily turn into an intractable affair.

The study of organizational effectiveness (OE) emerged in the 1960s as "an exciting construct" within the field of organizational behavior (Hirsch and Levin 1999, 200). By the late 1960s, however, OE was "a classical problem" in organizational scholarship, largely associated with goal achievement (Price 1968, 3). In the mid-1970s, researchers looked more seriously into the validity of the OE construct – which seemed intuitively coherent, but proved impossible to define or operationalize (Shenhav, Shrum and Alon 1994). Despite these problems, Cameron and Whetten, reflecting on two decades and hundreds of articles (and book chapters) on the topic, noted that the organizational effectiveness construct was "at the very center" of existing organizational models (Cameron and Whetten (Eds.) 1983, 1).

From the 1960s through the 1980s, the various conceptualizations of organizational effectiveness that were developed rarely overlapped, and regrettably, no consensus could be found on exactly what constituted organizational effectiveness (K. S. Cameron 1978) (Hirsch and Levin 1999, 201). Some scholars came to believe that a consensus on OE was impossible, and a "validity police" position emerged (e.g., Goodman, Atkin, and Schoorman

(1983, 166)) which argued for a halt to, or pull back from, studies of an umbrella construct. Other scholars argued that organizational effectiveness was not researchable, and should be retained only as a conceptually, rather than an empirically, relevant construct (Hannan and Freeman 1977). Kahn noted that the majority view among researchers was to retain the OE construct, but to try to give it a better definition and theoretical basis (Kahn 1977, 238). Goodman, Atkin, and Schoorman (1983, 175) called for a moratorium on studies of organizational effectiveness, expecting (correctly) that this would result in investigations of other indicators of performance, including satisfaction, productivity, and accidents, but not effectiveness. Reflecting a growing pessimism during the 1980s, Zammuto (1982, 48) noted that the question of organizational effectiveness had characteristics of a "wicked problem," in that the major challenge involved formulating the problem itself.

By the 1990s, emphasis had largely shifted away from theory toward the provision of practical descriptions of best practices for managers, along with calls for more relevance in business schools. Discussions of effectiveness that had been criticized earlier by practitioners as being too ethereal or theoretical, became discussions of effectiveness that were criticized by scholars as too pragmatic, thin, or over-simplified (e.g., Scott (1992)). Since the early 2000s, leading OE scholars have moved in a new direction – investigating positive deviance through positive organizational scholarship (POS). This is an effort to learn from highly positive outcomes, processes and attributes of organizations (Cameron, Dutton and Quinn 2003).

Today, however, the continuing lack of a defined concept for organizational effectiveness constrains organizational and management theory in significant ways. A confirmed concept of organizational effectiveness would be a major advance, and could be transformational due to the foundational role of OE within organization and management theory.

Drawing on three separate traditions to create a new synthesis

Theoretical concepts make up the basic building blocks of science, and represent phenomena in the "real world" that are being explained by a theory. A concept is an abstraction derived from observation of several specific cases. The important term here is 'observation,' as it provides a direct connection between the concept (the abstraction) and its referent (the reality) (Watt and Van Den Berg 1995, 11). The lack of an objective referent that can be observed in the field has led scholars to categorize organizational effectiveness as a vague *construct* rather than a defined *concept*.

To illustrate the difference between a construct and a concept, consider an elephant. We all know what an elephant looks like, and if required, could visit a site where an elephant was said to be present to verify its existence. Thus, an elephant exists as a concept because it has an objective referent (its physical appearance). Unfortunately, OE does not pass the same test under current theory. Scholars have not pointed to anything that can be observed in the field that will objectively verify organizational effectiveness; thus, it remains a theoretical construct (i.e., not directly observable).

Our synthesis of organizational effectiveness theory is based on a model (proposed by the author) that pairs a defined concept of OE to its objective referent in the real world, overcoming a key limitation of the past. The model draws on three separate traditions in different fields to develop a new and easily understood concept of organizational effectiveness. The three traditions are: (1) organizational scholarship, dealing with the nature of organizations, as well as their effectiveness, (2) quality management – first practiced in the automobile industry for defect reduction, but eventually leading to total quality management (TQM) for products and services, and agile methods for project management, and (3) results-based management (RBM), including logical frameworks and associated logic models — as practiced in international development projects. On first reading, this may seem an unlikely combination of ideas, but stay with me as a unifying framework unfolds.

Parallels between the traditions of organizational scholarship and quality management have been recognized for some time, as both traditions seek to improve organizational performance. When new articles and books on organizational effectiveness began to wane in the mid-1980s due to a challenge to the OE construct's validity, the literature on quality management was ascendant. For practitioners, 'quality' became the *summum bonum* relative to organizational performance (Cameron and Whetten 1996, 281).

The relevance of results-based management (our third tradition) to the problem of organizational effectiveness has become evident only recently. This tradition comes to us from international development, and offers ideas to improve the effectiveness of certain temporary organizations embodied in 'aid' projects and programs. Importantly, this last tradition may help supply a missing piece to the puzzle of organizational effectiveness, and its relevance to OE is being described here for the first time, due to the author's involvement in international development.

If a new view of effectiveness is to gain acceptance, it must offer an improved way to specify the concept — a way that overcomes or avoids problems of the past. In an overview chapter for a book on organizational effectiveness, Kahn (1977, 236) mused that "to be effective is merely to have effects." The main issue for Kahn was what effects were to be mapped to the concept of organizational effectiveness. If agreement on that issue could be reached, the problem would be solved; unfortunately, Kahn noted that such agreement did not exist, and he was left with a mix of "concepts, operations, criticisms, and objections."

Our new view of effectiveness is specified in the outcome-focused model (OFM) of OE, and forms the basis for Management by Positive Organizational Effectiveness (M+OE). The OFM looks at effectiveness in a new way, stating that the goal of every organization is to be effective within its environment. Like Kahn, the new model holds that 'effects' lie at the heart of its concept of effectiveness, and a set of outcome-level effects are defined as markers for OE.

First, we need to be clear about the meaning of the word 'outcome.' While it is in common English usage, it is important to distinguish between a general understanding of the term, and its specific meaning within the OFM. When the word 'outcome' is commonly used, it is seldom defined, but it generally confers one of two meanings, either the way a thing turns out (i.e., the final result), or an effect caused by an antecedent event. These two definitions are not necessarily compatible in each situation, which can lead to confusion. The OFM follows the second definition, in that an outcome is viewed as an effect brought about by an antecedent (and is not taken as a final result).

The outcome-focused model (OFM) equates effectiveness with the achievement of "expected external outcomes" (EEOs). In this context, an outcome is a relevant behavior by demand-side actors (outside the organization) that signifies the uptake, adoption or use of an organization's supply-side offerings (i.e., its outputs). A defined results chain is used to detail an organization's specific intentions to serve its environment through an offering, thus providing a hypothesis about how supply-side inputs and outputs bring about demand-side effects that include immediate outcomes and longer-term impacts. A results chain and its embedded hypothesis are validated by observing the achievement of expected external outcomes just outside the organization's boundary. For "uptake, adoption or use" to serve as a marker for effectiveness, however, it must occur in line with the result-chain logic for which the offering was created. Anything else would be reason to question the validity of the logic or the behavior. For example, if household latrines are used for storing hay (rather than their intended use), the causal logic of the results chain for a South Asian government's latrine program has *not* been shown to be effective.

Under the OFM, the basic problem of effectiveness is that a supply-side push from an offering must be met by a demand-side pull initiated by actors in the environment (otherwise, effectiveness is not present). Due to its behavioral and uncertain nature, the handoff from the supply-side push of the outputs to the pull of the expected outcomes is the weakest link in a defined results chain. Thus, the inability of the chain to induce expected external outcomes is the most likely reason for its failure.

Some may wonder whether I am claiming that all outcomes must have a behavioral component. No, only that the "expected external outcomes" (or EEOs used in the OFM) have been defined that way. Selecting an EEO for use in the results chain is an art, not a science, but I have never seen a case in which a relevant behavior could not be found. If done properly, EEOs are both behavioral in nature and readily observable in the field.

When demand-side actors adopt and use an offering, it is in the expectation of accruing economic, social, and other benefits for themselves by utilizing the product, service, or other offering over time. In return, an organization receives financial, social, and other benefits from these same actors and others within the environment — benefits that can serve to sustain internal processes, power growth, and provide a premium for effectiveness. It is the demand side that controls initiation of the interchange, however, thus an organization must always seek new and better ways to serve its environment (i.e., to generate and sustain expected outcome-level behaviors).

I will explain the outcome-focused model in more detail later in this chapter, but let us now consider three traditions that the model draws upon for its construction.

Organizational scholarship (Tradition 1): Drawing upon open-system contingency models

Early scholars emphasized ideal organizational forms and approaches where organizations were viewed as largely closed-systems. Efficiency was valued as the primary measure of effectiveness, and little need was assumed for interaction with the external environment (K. S. Cameron 2010, xiv). Over time, these early views gave way to open-system models that acknowledged environmental contingencies, and effectiveness was signified by the closeness of the match between the organization's attributes and its environment. Eventually, a third shift was reported in which scholars began studying transactions involving multiple stakeholders operating across the organization's boundaries (K. S. Cameron 2010, xv). Effective organizations were expected to have accurate information about the expectations and demands of key stakeholders, and to deliver on them. Effectiveness then required learning, adaptability, strategic intent, competitive positioning, and responsiveness.

From the 1970s onward, five models of organizational effectiveness have retained the most prominence in organizational scholarship (K. S. Cameron 2005, 308):

The goal model. Organizations are effective to the extent that they achieve their stated goals. Shareholder value creation has been a prominent goal for many organizations, yet other formal and informal goals have been used (e.g., profitability in business).

The system resource model. Organizations are effective to the extent that they acquire necessary resources. In this model, the external environment must be managed in a way to capture key and critical resources needed for survival.

The internal congruence or efficiency model. Organizations are effective to the extent that their internal functioning is consistent, efficiently organized, and functions with little strain.

The human relations model. Organizations are effective to the extent that they are healthy systems for the individuals who work in them. The emphasis is on engaging members, developing human resources, and providing a collaborative climate.

The multiple constituencies model. Organizations are effective to the extent that they satisfy their dominant stakeholders or their strategic constituencies, that is, the constituencies that have the most power relative to the organization.

Scholars point out that none of these models (nor any other available so far) applies to all settings. Each has its own strengths and focus. None can be substituted directly for the others in assessments, although combinations of criteria have been found in some studies. None offers an objective referent in a bounded concept space. Debates about which of these models is best are often irrelevant, because the models are more likely to complement each other rather than compete with one another (K. S. Cameron 1986, 541). Over the years, scholars have come to believe that a single theory cannot explain organizational effectiveness and that the leading models are useful in different circumstances (Morgan 1980) (Cameron and Whetten (Eds.) 1983, 274).

Organizational effectiveness has received less attention in recent years due to the confusion that remains (Whetten 2004), its relevance brought into question by the 'validity police' (Hirsch and Levin 1999) who dismiss the OE construct as non-specific and unworkable. Attempts to replace the term in the literature have resulted in growing emphasis on single indicators such as productivity, share price, financial ratios, customer loyalty, error rates, and the like (Cameron and Whetten 1996).

Despite the continued inability of scholars to define a valid OE *concept*, organizational effectiveness remains a *construct* critical to organizational evaluation. For example, school districts need to know which schools to revamp or close because of low educational success. Likewise, nonprofit organizations need to demonstrate to outside donors the effectiveness of funded programs, and businesses need to evaluate the effectiveness of recent initiatives. While scholars have come to believe that the OE construct is an enigma (K. S. Cameron 1981), and manifests characteristics of a "wicked problem" (Zammuto 1982, 48), leaders of organizations plow ahead trying to improve effectiveness using their own internal definitions of the term. Thus, the need for a clear concept — it is needed in one way or another every day — yet the existing tracks within organizational scholarship seem to have reached an impasse.

I will mention here that the outcome-focused model incorporates traditions from open-system contingency models (i.e., Tradition 1 in its formulation), but draws on other fields as well to formulate a new concept of organizational effectiveness (see below).

Quality management (Tradition 2): Adopting Standards and Continuous Improvement

Quality as a substitute for effectiveness. Cameron and Whetten (1996) noted that the most frequent substitute for effectiveness, and the construct most responsible for dramatic shifts in effectiveness research in recent decades, has been the 'quality' construct. Whereas 'effectiveness' has largely disappeared from the organizational studies literature since the mid-1980s, hundreds of articles and books have been published on quality after 1985 as the quality construct has evolved over the years.

In the beginning, quality was treated as a reliability engineering (or statistical control) issue and appeared mainly in engineering, operations management, and applied statistics literatures. It was primarily about reducing the variability of processes, thus reducing or eliminating defects in products and services. Largely limited in its application to production processes, it did not address overall organizational performance. Garvin (1988) identifies four "quality eras" in the United States: (1) an inspection era; (2) a statistical control era; (3) a quality assurance era; and (4) a strategic quality management era. The shift from the first era to the fourth era was largely a shift toward total quality management (TQM), or just 'quality management' in the USA. It is the TQM use of quality that has appeared in the organizational studies literature and rivals effectiveness as the key organizational-level dependent variable (Cameron and Whetten 1996, 265). W. Edwards Deming is often cited as the father of the TQM movement (Best and Neuhauser 2005). Over time, 'quality' has been appropriated to mean far more than its dictionary definition, and has become synonymous with a quality movement that has captured the imagination of the leaders of large corporations in the US and abroad (e.g., GE, Boeing, Caterpillar, Ford).

So far, the quality literature has been written largely by practitioners, as opposed to academic scholars. This is likely due to its roots. The quality movement began in manufacturing, most famously in the automobile industry in Japan, thus it has largely concentrated upon the practical problems of getting the job done. Prior to the late

1980s, the scholarly literature treated quality as a predictor of effectiveness, and was seen as a desirable attribute (among others) of an organization's offerings (Cameron and Whetten 1996, 280-281). Quality was defined in different ways by different gurus and practitioners, and the various definitions existed primarily in the minds of the definers (K. S. Cameron 1981), thus no one view was considered completely correct (Cameron and Whetten 1996, 283). Like organizational effectiveness, quality lacked an objective referent and was a construct rather than a concept. TQM practices, such as Deming's 14 points, were often viewed as useful prescriptive principles, but lacked a theoretical frame that explained the underlying mechanisms at work. Some scholars have subsequently offered theory to explain the relevant mechanisms underlying TQM (Anderson, Rungtusanatham and Schroeder 1994) (Dean and Bowen 1994).

Despite the drawbacks mentioned above, a switch to quality (as reflected in TQM) seemed to remove certain impediments that had hampered effectiveness research; impediments such as: (1) discord among different approaches to effectiveness, (2) a lack of integration between processes and results, and (3) a lack of emphasis on organizational culture (Cameron and Whetten 1996, 285).

Quality's harmonization of models. Cameron and Whetten (1996, 285) noted that comprehensive approaches to quality (e.g., TQM) help to harmonize models of effectiveness. For example, consider OE models such as the goal model, the internal congruence or efficiency model, the system resource model, the human resources model, and the strategic constituencies model. Discussions in the literature regarding which model best represents organizational realities have been intense in the past (Seashore and Yuchtman 1967) (Price 1972) (Steers 1975) (Bluedorn 1980) (Connolly, Conlon and Deutsch 1980) (Quinn and Rohrbaugh 1981). Yet the TQM approach to quality appears to harmonize each of these models appropriately. That is, the key attributes of quality include such things as the production of defect-free products and services and the continuous improvement of objectives (goal model), the adoption of processes and practices that ensure smooth, efficient organizational functioning (internal processes model), the integration of suppliers and resource providers into the planning, design, and budgeting of products and services (system resource model), the provision of a supportive environment for employees to work (the human resources model), and the satisfaction of customers (multiple constituencies model). TQM embraces each of these attributes as being necessary and interdependent in the achievement of high levels of performance. While traditional debates on OE highlight differences among the models and the advantages of one perspective over another, a focus on TQM fosters an integration of divergent perspectives under a broad umbrella (Cameron and Whetten 1996, 285).

Quality's integration of processes and results. A second apparent advantage of quality over effectiveness is that it integrates methods and tools for accomplishing quality along with desired organizational results. An inherent part of the construct itself is the assumption that particular processes and procedures are in operation in quality organizations to drive the production of desired outputs. Unlike most OE models, 'quality' almost always includes methods, practices, and systems along with organizational results and effects – as it appears to be more encompassing of means and ends than is effectiveness (Cameron and Whetten 1996, 287).

Quality's comprehensiveness. A third advantage to quality, related to the two above, is that it may have a comprehensiveness advantage over effectiveness. Quality is treated as an 'organizational culture,' that is, as a paradigm, a set of values, a way of approaching work and people.

In the TQM sense, it represents a peculiar organizational mind-set in addition to being a set of processes and results. It may, therefore, represent a broader construct than the one typical of the effectiveness literature (Cameron and Whetten 1996, 289).

While some advantages of quality over effectiveness have been noted, effectiveness appears to have advantages over quality as a construct of choice for organizational studies (Cameron and Whetten 1996, 293). These advantages relate to: (1) the prescriptive and normative nature of quality, (2) problems with customer preferences and customer satisfaction, and (3) a lack of conceptual bounding of quality. Cameron & Whetten argued that future research into OE should provide more emphasis on the integration and linkage of processes, results, and effects. Instead of focusing primarily on results, effectiveness research needed to give more attention to process criteria, how results are produced, as well as what is produced — together with evident consequences (Cameron and Whetten 1996, 300).

How the OFM is like 'quality,' but surpasses it. The outcome-focused model, like quality, serves to harmonize prominent OE models by showing how they are part of a larger, all-encompassing concept (discussed later in this chapter). In addition, the OFM links processes, results, and effects within defined results chains, thus gaining advantages like those that the quality construct enjoys. The outcome-focused model goes beyond quality, however, when it pairs a defined concept of organizational effectiveness with an objective referent (expected external outcomes, or EEOs, which can be empirically observed in the field). The OFM incorporates aspects of TQM as Tradition 2 in its formulation in order to implement process standards (e.g., positive values, guaranteed attributes, and defect-free production in its offerings), and enable continuous improvement methods (including agile techniques).

Results-based management (Tradition 3): Focusing on outcomes

The third tradition being drawn upon for the OFM is Results-based Management, an approach to project and program planning which began as an attempt to improve effectiveness in certain temporary organizations (i.e., 'aid' projects). It is often associated with the 'logical framework' (or logframe), logical framework approach (LFA), logic models, and the theory of change (NORAD 1999) (Asian Development Bank 2006) (Kellogg Foundation 2004) (Wholey, Hatry and Newcomer (Eds.) 2010). These techniques incorporate a hierarchy of objectives and/or results chain within a logframe matrix, where this story begins.

The early history of the 'logframe' is somewhat murky, but its use in the development community began in the late-1960s in USAID. From there it spread to other development agencies, and it has now been used in varying forms by most international development agencies since the late 1990s – including the multi-lateral development banks, UN Agencies, bilateral aid donors, NGOs, and some aid-recipient countries. The relevance for our purposes is that aid projects and programs are temporary organizations that have many of the characteristics of organizations everywhere (e.g., inputs, activities, outputs, and higher-level objectives). The effectiveness of aid (which is often composed of a wide variety of grant and loan initiatives in different sectors of an emerging economy) has been a recurring topic for decades, and the use of the RBM/logframe techniques can be seen as an effort by the aid community to inoculate itself against, if not cure, the disease of aid ineffectiveness.

Like the tradition of quality, the literature describing the use of RBM (and related techniques) has arisen from the practitioner community rather than from academic scholars. As might be expected, it is light on theory and heavy on practice. It is the structured nature of the practice (specifically, its primary focus on outcomes within a hierarchy of objectives), that has something to offer the OFM and its concept of organizational effectiveness. Rather than offering 'how-to' commentary on RBM (including LFA & logframe practice), I will primarily concentrate on aspects of the techniques that may offer an important missing piece to the concept of organizational effectiveness within the OFM.

Figure 7.1
The Logical Framework of Results-Based Management(RBM)

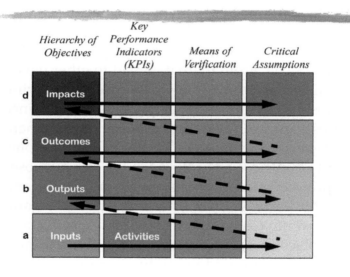

First, a brief outline of the logical framework is necessary to understand RBM. A logical framework (Figure 7.1) has four levels that make up a hierarchy of objectives. Beginning at the bottom, the four vertical levels include (a) inputs (and activities), (b) outputs, (c) outcomes, and (d) impacts. A results chain within the logical framework links the four levels and provides a hypothesis regarding how results will be produced by the project (i.e., the temporary organization). According to the logic, resources (inputs) are converted to activities, activities produce outputs (given certain assumptions), outputs achieve outcomes (given certain assumptions), and finally, outcomes generate impacts over time (longer-term effects in society, given certain assumptions).

How the Outcome-focused Model (OFM) differs from Results Based Management (RBM)

While the OFM uses the hierarchy of objectives from RBM, it differs from it because the OFM divides supply from demand. As shown in Figure 7.2, the OFM considers *inputs* (plus *activities*) and *outputs* to be on the supply side (within the control of the organization), while *outcomes* and *impacts* are on the demand side (outside the control of the organization). The RBM does not make this distinction, but rather considers outcomes to come in multiple varieties, including intermediate and final outcomes. This leads to confusion in RBM between outputs and outcomes, since the intermediate outcomes of RBM may well be under the control of the organization.

The most important level for evaluating effectiveness under the OFM is the outcome level, which contains the outcome-level effects (& associated EEOs). Under the OFM, outcomes should not be viewed as the final result, but rather effects verified by the observation of relevant behaviors that signify the uptake, adoption or use of the offerings by external actors (in line with the result-chain logic). OFM outcomes are the weakest link in a defined results chain due to their behavioral component, yet their achievement implies the validity of the embedded causal hypothesis and the expected completion of the entire results chain.

Figure 7.2
Results chain logic of the Outcome-focused Model (OFM)

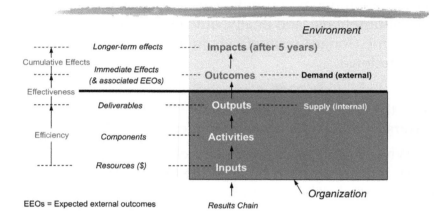

EEOs = Expected external outcomes

In adapting the RBM approach to the outcome-focused model, I have qualified my outcome terminology for clarity by using the phrase "expected external outcomes" (or EEOs) to signify that they occur at the interface between the organization and its environment, but outside the direct control of the organization. This may seem like a small point, but it turns out to be pivotal – as the EEOs provide the objective referent for our concept of OE. The designation of the supply/demand interface as the boundary between outputs/outcomes and organization/environment is probably the most significant contribution of the OFM (distinguishing it from RBM practice). Conveniently, the supply/demand interface offers the best place to directly observe EEOs as a marker for effectiveness. When Figure 7.2 refers to 'immediate effects' at the outcome level, it means immediate effects <u>after</u> the outputs are complete and demand-side actors have been given access to them.

An OFM outcome is not achieved until a favorable external response (or EEO) is verified in the form of the uptake, adoption, or use by the beneficiaries, customers, or other target groups (in line with the results chain logic). It is not enough to produce high quality infrastructure or services that no one is willing to use, maintain, or pay for (depending upon the logic). To be judged effective, an initiative must generate an expected response that signifies demand-side success.

For instance, an agricultural extension project operating under the OFM would be judged effective only if the local farmers adopt and use a new package of farming techniques being offered by the project. The farmers are outside the direct control of the project and are not being paid to be a part of its initiatives, although they may receive some training along the way. Thus, farmers are unlikely to adopt a new package of farming techniques (a project output) unless they clearly see the benefits, believe that the chances for their success are high, and that the costs are affordable. The results chain of the project intervention will be designed to foster in the farmers the expected voluntary behaviors required for success. If the farmers do not adopt the expected new behaviors, the results chain fails and the project is judged 'ineffective.'

The logical framework approach (LFA) evolved to its modern form by incorporating *participatory* design techniques, for instance, involving the target farmers and other stakeholders at an early stage of the design process to help develop key features of the project.

Finally, the highest level of the hierarchy (the impact level) takes account of longer-term spread effects expected broadly in society because of a successful initiative, perhaps at the regional or national levels. Examples such as "brand identity" or "firm reputation" come to mind at the impact level in a broader organizational context. This is also where true greatness lies within the context of M+OE. Impacts represent longer-term manifestations of immediate outcomes sustained over time and are thus a cumulative view of effectiveness, rather than an instantaneous one. It is not the direct responsibility of a project initiative to achieve or document achievements at the impact-level (as they will only be available sometime after project completion), but this level is provided at the top of the logical framework to provide high-level logic regarding the expected longer-term effects of the intervention and to guide future evaluators who may visit the field up to five years or so after completion of the initiative to look at these and other effects.

Thousands of development projects have incorporated RBM/LFA/OFM techniques over the years (and continue to do so), although different agencies have implemented the approach in different ways, using somewhat different definitions of terms. The most common problem with the technique has been maintaining high standards of quality during the process, since the logical framework itself is difficult to do well (i.e., with defensible logic) but easy to do poorly (e.g., by just filling in the boxes). For a development agency, a choice must be made between training all staff in how to create a logical framework, or at least to understand its use (which most agencies have tried), or providing a more formal process – together with help desk staffed by logframe experts — to ensure quality. The most successful adherents seem to be those agencies that introduce quality processes and a professional help desk to ensure that the techniques are being used properly.

Having briefly outlined the OFM model and covered the three traditions that have been tapped to form its basis, I will focus on the underlying nature of organizations used as the foundation for the OFM.

The organization as an intentional actor

Concepts of organizational effectiveness are built on precepts that provide an underlying view of the organization itself. The first precept in the outcome-focused model is that "the organization is usefully understood as a particular kind of social actor, capable of behaving in a purposeful, intentional manner" (King, Felin and Whetten 2010, 291). The organizational actor concept, as distinct from cultural and market-like forces, was emphasized by Coleman (1990) (1991), who studied the growth of purposefully established organizations and noted their significant influence on the social environment. Two theoretical assumptions give substance to the concept of the organization as actor.

First, an external attribution assumption holds that organizations must be attributed by other actors as being capable of acting, especially their primary stakeholders and audiences (King, Felin and Whetten 2010, 292). Organizations are legitimate actors because that status is granted by society, not only legally, but practically and linguistically as well. Such status is conferred by the expectations of others, who monitor and hold organizations accountable for their actions (Bauman and May 2001) (Czarniawska 1997).

Second, an intentionality assumption holds that actors "are capable of deliberation, self-reflection, and goal-directed action" (King, Felin and Whetten 2010, 292). This assumption is based on the social psychology of action and motivation (e.g., Deci & Ryan (1985)) and the philosophy of the mind (Dennett 1987), together with organizational research on decision making (Gavetti, Levinthal and Ocasio 2007). Organizations can be viewed as intentional actors because the organization's member-agents are guided by an organizational self-view that guides their choices and directs their behavior. Without this internal sense of direction and self-reflection, the actions of an organization would not be attributable to a source other than the individuals making up the organization or the environment where the organization is embedded (King, Felin and Whetten 2010, 292).

Organizations do more than simply occupy a role in society, they are mechanisms for its change. They become actors that exert influence on individuals, shape communities, and transform their environments (King, Felin and Whetten 2010, 292). In short, organizations are like other actors in society such as individuals and the state, and because they are actors, they are different from other social forms such as markets or communities (King, Felin and Whetten 2010, 292).

In summary, our first precept holds that organizations are independent actors because society grants them that status, and over time, organizations gain a self-view accumulated from their emergent, path-dependent personalities and enduring qualities (Selznick 1949) (Selznick 1957) (Stinchcombe 1965) that allows them to formulate intentions that direct their actions.

The organization serves its environment, and is rewarded in return

The second precept to be stipulated as part of the OFM is that an organization is an economic and social entity that exists to accomplish something outside of itself, that is, to create, amplify and channel economic, social, and other benefits in its environment. Our claim is that an organization does not exist simply to do something for itself (e.g., profit), but rather to serve its environment (e.g., society as a whole, or a segment of society).

In a well-known passage from the *Wealth of Nations*, Adam Smith notes that "it is not from the benevolence of the butcher, the brewer or the baker that we expect our dinner, but from their regard to their own interest" (Smith [1776] 2005, 19). Generations have taken Smith's words to mean that the purpose of a firm is to satisfy private interests and maximize profit (Amaeshi, Nnodim and Osuji 2013,

9), but this view only serves as a shiny object that diverts our attention and should not be the main conclusion. It is more important to realize that neither the butcher, the brewer, nor the baker would be in business for long if their purposes did not serve the interests and needs of society. Smith notes in a later passage that "the butcher, the brewer, and the baker…together with many other artificers and retailers necessary or useful for supplying their occasional wants… contribute still further to augment the town. The inhabitants of the town, and those of the country, are mutually the servants of one another" (Smith [1776] 2005, 309).

Thus, I contend that the purpose of a firm is not to satisfy private interests nor to maximize profits, but rather to create, amplify, and channel benefits in society so that the firm can receive benefits due to it in return. Observe that markets primarily involve voluntary exchanges in which firms offer value to society and receive benefits in return as compensation. This is the environment in which an effective firm (and more generally, an effective organization) will find its place.

Let us consider what it would mean for an organization to exist as an intentional and value-offering actor whose objective is to be effective within its environment. Such an organization seeks to create offerings that can provide benefits to, and meet the needs of, selected external actors. Through its offerings, the organization is expecting to induce benefit exchanges with external actors in the environment. A transfer of benefits begins once an expected external outcome (behavior) is observed, but this process is not within the organization's control.

Organizations cannot directly initiate the transfer of benefits through internal processes, since external actors are not under their direction. It is up to the external actors themselves to decide that the organization's offerings are sufficiently useful or desirable to compel outcome-level behaviors (such as the uptake, adoption or use of the offerings — at prevailing prices, as applicable). This notion is akin to what economists call 'consumer sovereignty.' Within a results chain of the OFM, the internal supply-side push from the organization (i.e., offering outputs) must be converted to a demand-side pull by external actors (i.e., the outcome-level behaviors of uptake, adoption, or use) if effectiveness is to occur and be verified through observation. This is the challenge of effectiveness.

Outcome-level behaviors are initiated by external actors in an effort to accrue financial, economic, social, psychological, spiritual, and environmental benefits for themselves (e.g., through use of and engagement with an organization's offerings over time). Such benefits accrue to society (and the environment) as a whole, since external actors are a part of society. At the same time and in exchange for the above, these same actors (and perhaps others) bestow financial, social, and other types of benefits on the organization — benefits that are typically distributed among stakeholders such as owners, employees, suppliers, and other partners. Thus, our second precept is expected to motivate behavior on two levels: benefits that accrue within the environment can motivate key elements of society to welcome and support the organization's presence and growth, while benefits that accrue to the organization can be used to motivate internal stakeholders regarding their own interests.

A hierarchy of benefits can be formulated with respect to exchanges between the organization and its environment (Figure 7.3): from the lower to higher, financial & economic, social & psychological, and environmental & spiritual. Financial & economic benefits were described earlier (Chapter 6) when transactions were involved. Social benefits occur when we establish increasing rapport with those around us. Psychological benefits occur when we feel better about ourselves. Spiritual benefits occur when we increase our respect for the wonder of our existence. Environmental benefits occur when we increase the health and resilience of the whole (common good), including the natural environment.

Chester Barnard explored social and psychological factors in his classic work, *The Functions of the Executive* (Barnard 1938). When organizations use M+OE and focus on environmental benefits that build up the whole, I believe that they become aware of, and gain access to, all the subordinate benefits within the hierarchy. I cannot point to empirical evidence that this is the case, but it is consistent with my observations. In a similar vein, a narrow focus on only the lower level transactional benefits (financial & economic) may well limit (or negate) the generation of benefits at higher levels. We explore benefit exchanges again in Chapter 13, with an example.

In addition to a range of benefits being exchanged, let's consider the capital accounts. Capital, in the traditional economic sense, was understood in 1900 as a durable result of past production processes, enabling future production while not being transformed itself, and part of a closed system that included land, labor and capital. It was associated with the capitalist as economic actor in the environment. When used in the production process, capital was expected to generate a flow of goods and services over time (Dean and Kretschmer 2007, 574-575).

To use capital in other ways (social, psychological, spiritual, & environmental) represents an extended or hybrid form and requires a new conceptualization of the traditional notion of capital. Hybrid capital is intangible, and its ownership may be ambiguous. It may not be associated with an economic actor, and can reside in the networks and relationships between individuals. Hybrid capital captures less measurable aspects of the production process to explain how seemingly identical processes (in terms of traditional factors of production) can yield markedly different results across organizations (Dean and Kretschmer 2007, 581). In an extension of the meaning of Figures 7.2 & 7.3, it seems logical to expect improved affinity and stability between the organization and its environment when the organization invests in the generation of social / psychological capital, and well as environmental / spiritual capital in the environment in a targeted manner.

Figure 7.3
Hierarchy of Benefits

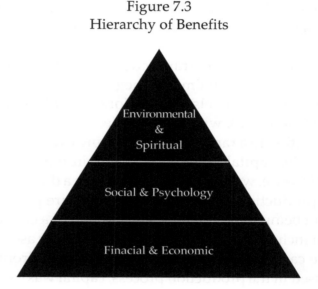

Generative Emergence

Today scholars often view organizations as networked, dynamical, nonlinear, and subject to evolutionary processes and adaptive pressures in a changing environment. They are complex adaptive systems that exhibit emergent properties that come from below through the interaction of internal agents (discussed in Chapter 4). Organizational trajectories may not follow smooth and predictable patterns congenial with aspects of the goal model.

A useful view of emergence for our purposes is captured by the idea of generative emergence, in which agents actively pursue the creation of something new (a product or service, project, or initiative), which drives the system into a state of disequilibrium. Tension increases as experiments (using various combinations of relevant attributes) are tried to find an offering that generates a positive response in the demand-side environment. At some point the system will reach a critical point in which the effort will either generate emergent demand or die in failure. The elements of disequilibrium, tension, experiments, and re-combination are present in all major studies that call on dissipative structures theory (Lichtenstein 2016).

A similar process is envisaged in the OFM, where a results chain outlines a causal sequence of steps expected for a successful new product introduction. EEOs delineate the expected demand-side behaviors that would signify uptake, adoption or use of the new supply-side offerings. As in generative emergence, internal agents experiment with different combinations of attributes in the package being offered to the environment. If a high degree of acceptance emerges for a specific new offering from demand-side actors, then the results chain may be judged initially effective (and the offering becomes a candidate for production scale up).

Advantages of the outcome-focused model

In the outcome-focused model (OFM), organizations are effective to the extent that they achieve expected external outcomes (EEOs) as a result of creating and managing internal processes which are outcome-focused. Like the quality construct, the outcome-focused model links processes to results and effects, but validates causality and necessary conditions through direct observation of results at each stage along the input-output/outcome-impact results chain. Logically, there can be no outputs without inputs, no outcomes without outputs, and no impacts without outcomes. Likewise, the supply-side push cannot be converted to a demand-side pull unless external actors recognize that a favorable benefit exchange is in the offing, and act as expected on that recognition.

The OFM is not inconsistent with earlier models, but rather provides a framework that allows previous models to be absorbed under the umbrella of the OFM. First, the OFM would temper the goal model by specifying that only outcome-level objectives and results should be considered relevant for effectiveness. It is the outcome level that defines the first external demand-side reaction (and weakest link) necessary to verify that the results chain is working. Other levels of the objective hierarchy are important, but they are not specifically about effectiveness. Observe that the initial link (Figure 7.2) from inputs (and activities) to outputs is under the control of the organization and is primarily about efficiency, while the final link from outcomes to impacts will be successful if expected external outcomes continue to be observed. Thus, it is only the link from outputs to outcomes that creates a significant unknown in the results sequence, and this is where effectiveness is expressed.

Under the OFM, each offering to the environment is evaluated separately for a favorable demand-side response. A finding of effectiveness is dependent on a favorable evaluation of the efficacy of the logic model (achievement of EEOs via the results chain) used to deliver individual initiatives of the organization. There is a large literature on program theory from the evaluation field. Program theory evaluations may consider intervention problems that are simple, complicated, or complex, together with expected outcomes that are linear, non-linear, or emergent (Rogers 2008).

In addition to the goal model, the other prominent models for organizational effectiveness are harmonized, and retain value, within the OFM framework. Their areas of focus can be expected to act as constraints on organizational effectiveness if they do not receive due attention. Within the context of the OFM, resources (as in the system resource model) are necessary to drive results chains so that outcome-level objectives can be achieved, and achievement of organizational effectiveness itself will generate significant resource inputs for survival by way of benefit exchanges with the environment. Internal processes must function efficiently (as in the internal congruence or efficiency model) and with minimal strain for results chains to function, and for effectiveness (and efficiency) to be achieved. Human relations represent an important internal focus area, and organizations need to provide healthy systems for the individuals who work in them (as in the human relations model) if organizational effectiveness is to be achieved and sustained.

The outcome-focused model recognizes that multiple constituencies must be satisfied (as in the multiple constituencies model), but the most critical constituency for effectiveness is composed of demand-side actors who are expected to adopt and use the outputs in order for the results chain(s) to be deemed effective. Interestingly, this constituency is self-selecting through its behavior, and elevates itself to preferential status without debate among scholars regarding which stakeholder group *should be* most highly regarded. The preferential status this constituency derives comes from the fact that no benefits (including inputs necessary for survival) would flow to the organization without the favorable actions (i.e., behaviors) of members of this constituency.

Within the outcome-focused model an organization must serve its environment (it is not optional), else it receives no benefits in return. Changes in the behavior of external actors can quickly increase or decrease OE, thus an organization must adapt in a timely way by recasting its offerings to remain relevant, even indispensable, to its environment. Naturally, there may be internal or external constraints on the ability or willingness of an organization and its leaders to adapt (Hannan and Freeman 1977, 931-932). Yet a Darwinian-style imperative is at work behind the scenes to enforce "survival of the effective." Over time, ineffective organizations are marginalized or eliminated in the absence of adequate benefit exchanges with their environment. Effective organizations, alternatively, are selectively retained to survive and thrive. Organizations that are highly effective for a period (e.g., Google) can experience rapid growth, and appear to enjoy an effectiveness premium through preferential benefit exchanges with actors in the environment. Effectiveness thus confers significant advantage when facing present and future challenges. Support for natural selection can be found in organizational studies literature, where Hannan and Freeman (1977) (1989) employed the concept.

Key points of the Outcome-focused Model (OFM) are as follows:

1. Organizations are economic and social entities that function as intentional actors to achieve purposes outside of themselves, that is, to create, amplify and channel benefits in their environment, including society as a whole.
2. The goal of every organization is the same, that is, to be effective within its environment. Effectiveness, when achieved and maintained through positive values, confers all that an organization needs to survive and thrive.

3. An organization is effective to the extent that it successfully converts its supply-side intentions to serve its environment (through specific offerings) into expected demand-side behaviors that signify uptake, adoption or use (of its offerings). These favorable behaviors are termed "expected external outcomes" (EEOs), because they are in line with the logic of the results chain and can be observed at the supply/demand interface, just outside the direct control of the organization itself.

4. Effective organizations survive and thrive on the strength of benefit exchanges with external actors in their environment. This process works to selectively boost (or hamper) an organization's prospects for retention in the environment based on the strength (or weakness) of exchanges with external actors, and enforces "survival of the effective." In return for serving its environment, an organization accrues benefits for itself – benefits that are distributed typically among owners, employers, suppliers, and other stakeholders, as applicable.

5. Economic, social, and other benefits accruing to the environment are not delivered directly by the organization as a result of its processes, but rather indirectly. External actors accrue such benefits for themselves as they adopt and use the organization's offerings for their own purposes. The demand-side remains in control of benefit exchange initiation, so that organizations must always seek new and better ways to serve their environment in the future.

6. Effectiveness is about converting the supply-side intentions of an organization into favorable demand-side responses in the external environment.

Results chains are used to describe the linkage between inputs & outputs on the supply side, and outcomes & impacts on the demand side. The strength of expected behaviors can and should be observed directly to verify effectiveness. Such behaviors provide the missing referent that is needed for a verifiable concept of organizational effectiveness.

7. Expected external outcomes observed within a defined results chain offer verification of effectiveness at the chain's weakest link (i.e., external behavioral response), thus suggesting that the entire results chain is valid. Expected external outcomes observed in the present provide the most relevant confirmation of effectiveness for management consideration. Note: it is more important to *verify* effectiveness through observation of behaviors (and to learn what drives their increase or decrease) than it is to *measure* effectiveness (as a meaningful scale may not be found in all cases).

8. Validated results chains are valuable assets of an organization (i.e., sources of competitive advantage), and provide opportunities for scale-up and growth.

9. Where outputs are produced without the achievement of their associated and expected external outcomes, the outputs are largely waste – because the defined results chain has failed and is, therefore, ineffective. If unintended positive benefits are found as part of program evaluation, however, they should be tested for replicability as part of a future results chain hypothesis.

10. Achieving organizational effectiveness in complex organizations (and organizational groupings) involves the management of a portfolio of offerings (each with its own results chain) in a way that

maximizes, or at least suffices, the achievement of expected external outcomes from the portfolio overall. In this way, overall effectiveness is optimized from the level of the individual offerings (addressed by the OFM) to the aggregate level of the portfolio overall (whether it be for one organization, or a group of organizations cooperating together).

11. The principles of organizational effectiveness can be used for good or for ill, depending upon the values that are expressed within organizational processes. Even a drug cartel can be effective, but effectiveness becomes negative when it breaks the law, or resorts to coercive and deceptive means to achieve its ends. Embedding an organization with positive values associated with virtuousness is a prerequisite for a journey toward greatness. "Be virtuous" is not just a nice thing to do, it embeds values necessary for high reliability.

12. The OFM contains a virtuous benefit cycle. Effectiveness is verified by observing demand-side behaviors. Such behaviors signify that use is taking place. Use means that benefits are being exchanged. Benefit exchanges mean that use is likely to continue. Once started, the virtuous cycle of effectiveness is likely to be sustained (unless disrupted by environmental change), leading to impact-level spread effects over time. Thus, a portfolio of effective offerings can be the engine of a great organization.

How often should organizations observe outcome-level behaviors to gauge effectiveness? That depends upon the organization, the nature of its products or services, and the frequency with which external actors can be expected to return in search of new offerings. In the case of a fast-food restaurant, short-term daily and weekly data are likely to be of interest; but in the case of an automobile dealership, monthly or quarterly data may be more relevant for judging effectiveness. Government organizations or non-profits will find a yearly evaluation most relevant. Despite the period established by management for data collection and/or observation, the OFM offers relevant outcome-level data any time one needs to observe the effectiveness of a defined results chain; it is only necessary to look for expected behaviors at the interface between the organization and its environment to verify effectiveness. Impact-level spread effects occur as outcomes are sustained over time in the OFM. The outcome-focused model thus responds to scholars who call for a clear explanation of time scales that pertain in theory development (Zaheer, Albert and Zaheer 1999).

This chapter has provided a relatively deep dive into the scholarly side of OE in an attempt to provide a new synthesis of OE theory. We use the new synthesis as a foundation for our concept of OE going forward. It also forms the basis for the OFM, and for our approach to M+OE. Subsequent chapters in the book will refer back to what is contained herein as we prepare to enter the Age of Organizational Effectiveness.

CHAPTER 8

IS A PARADIGM SHIFT UNDERWAY IN MANAGEMENT THOUGHT?

It was Thomas Kuhn in his 1962 book *The Structure of Scientific Revolutions* that popularized the idea of paradigm shifts in science (Kuhn 1962). The Copernican Revolution was one such shift. It had been a thousand years since Aristotle had said that the Universe revolved around the Earth, but in 1539 Copernicus said that no, in fact, the Earth revolves around the Sun (Copernicus [1543] 1995). His model was also better able to explain the anomaly's that were being seen in the heavens, particularly the irregular movements of planets like Mars and Venus. The new way of thinking was seen by the church as being in opposition to its teachings. In 1616, the Catholic Church banned Copernicus' book. In 1633, Galileo was convicted of heresy for his views, which were derived from years of direct observation of the heavens with his telescopes. It was not until 1835 that the church fully removed the prohibitions associated with the Copernican revolution (some three hundred years).

Paradigm shifts can take a while to work themselves out. Thomas Kuhn noted that they occur in phases. First, the pre-paradigm phase occurs in which there is no consensus, and several incompatible or incomplete theories compete with one another. In the second phase, a new way of thinking emerges which can solve a number of puzzles within a single mental framework or paradigm. In this phase, normal science can be conducted using the paradigm, and the main ideas are working well. Eventually anomalies appear that cannot be accommodated by the paradigm, marking the potential end of the second phase. In the third phase, the anomalies have failed to be resolved and a new type of science emerges from a different direction (Kuhn 1962).

These days, whenever one starts talking about a paradigm shift, critics may accuse you of using the latest buzz words. In 2012, Steve Denning (in *Forbes*) wrote about a paradigm shift that he believed was happening in management, and received just such a reaction (S. Denning 2012). The new paradigm he described involved an approach called "Radical Management" (S. Denning 2011a), where the purpose of a firm is focused on delighting customers instead of creating profit for the owners. He contrasted Radical Management with the traditional management model, which he noted was still largely based on Frederick Taylor's *Scientific Management* (Taylor [1911] 1998). Taylor first introduced management systems to make employees into "first-class men" and to improve the efficiency of the firm.

The basic idea of traditional management is that firms make money for their owners. Managers control the individuals in the firm, and a bureaucracy introduces rules, plans, and reports to create a predictable and stable organization. This is all in the service of efficiency and productivity (i.e., instrumentality). When things go awry, managers introduce cost-cutting and downsizing. This is basically a top-down command-and-control model using bureaucratic systems. All the principles are self-reinforcing and interlocking. Denning notes that since Taylor's day, overlays have been added for such things as industrial relations, human relations, organizational behavior and systems, human resource development, human resource management and employee relations, to name a few; but the same basic model (based on Taylor) remains in place today. It is largely driven by a belief in management's ability to set goals and to drive performance within the organization.

In Denning's new Radical Management paradigm, the manager's job is to enable self-organizing teams to delight the customer. Denning believes that the customer is in control now because he/she can go elsewhere very easily. There are so many choices and so much overcapacity, particularly in the manufacturing sector, that the customer can be picky.

While I agree with the need to delight the customer, I see a broader purpose for a new-style organization, one where the organization serves its environment and is rewarded in return. Within the environment there are a variety of actors, including customers and non-customers, as well as a multitude of other organizations in business, government, and nonprofit sectors. An idea like "shared value," proposed by Michael Porter and Mark Kramer, is only one possibility when an organization starts to look around its environment to actively explore how best to serve it. Managers can become facilitators to empower self-organizing teams around the design and delivery of a variety of current and future offerings.

Much of what Denning is talking about came out of the so-called 'agile' movement which started by focusing on the improvement of software project implementation using self-organizing teams, 'scrum' techniques, and scheduled meetings every couple of weeks to discuss progress. Scrum teams engage in sprints, with short bursts to achieve something and then report back. Agile principles and practices seem to work well in software development, where they started, but many of the agile techniques have recently expanded into wider business settings (Denning, Goldstein and Pacanowsky 2015). It should be noted that agile methods for project management are broadly part of the quality movement, and have much in common with TQM methods for products and services (Chapter 7).

We are still in Kuhn's Phase 1 when it comes to the adoption of agile methods outside of software production. It is too early to say that a paradigm shift has taken hold in management thought to enable wide-spread adoption. As mentioned above, Taylor's methods are still dominant in most of the economy (i.e., in Kuhn's Phase 2, normal science), although they are not working as well as in the past (anomalies emerging?). The nature of firms being what they are, and business schools being what they are, it is very hard for a new paradigm to make inroads rapidly. Among business schools, we are more likely to see the emergence of new schools of thought that remain largely separate from the main stream until they prove their worth. Among practitioners, individual organizations are free to adopt whatever management practices they desire, firm by firm, but that too would not provide the evidence necessary to confirm a paradigm shift in the short-term. Despite the flicker of new ideas on the horizon, we can only hope that management thought doesn't take 300 years to confirm a new paradigm, as in the Copernicium revolution.

CHAPTER 9

DOES "SHARED VALUE" REINVENT CAPITALISM?

Michael Porter and Mark Kramer introduced "shared value" as the next big idea to reinvent capitalism (Porter and Kramer 2011). In this chapter, we consider whether it has lived up to its original promise. According to Porter & Kramer, capitalism is under siege, and business has been viewed by some as a major cause of social, environmental, and economic problems.

The basic idea of shared value is that through cooperation between business and non-profit sectors, economic value can be created in a way that also includes value for society — creating social value along with economic value. Porter & Kramer believe that companies have been trapped in an outdated model of value creation and that they have been optimizing short term financial performance in a bubble, while missing the most important customer needs. They suggest that companies should take the lead to bring business and society back together. Shared value initiatives should not be relegated to the margins, they note, but should be at the center of what companies do. It is about reconceiving the intersection between society and corporate performance. Some companies have already embraced it, the authors write, including GE, Google, IBM, Intel, Johnson & Johnson, Nestle, Unilever, and Walmart (Porter and Kramer 2011).

In a somewhat related approach that predates shared value by many decades, the corporate social responsibility (CSR) movement has gained momentum in recent times. CSR is about redistributing some of the value that business had already created to nonprofits and others through philanthropy efforts, so CSR is certainly not the same as shared value (which is more about the co-creation of value going forward). The scope and boundary of CSR is still debated among scholars. At one extreme is the view of the noted economist Milton Friedman, who argued that business has no specific obligation under CSR (but only to maximize profit) (Friedman 1970). Other scholars claim that the CSR obligations of business have economic, legal, ethical, and philanthropic dimensions (Center for Ethical Business Cultures 2010). Porter & Kramer have offered shared value because CSR alone does not offer a solution to society's ills.

We will consider some examples of shared value in this chapter, but let's try to understand the basic idea before we get there. Porter believes that the true purpose of the corporation is really to create shared value and not just profit per se. He views shared value as the best chance to legitimize business again. It is about implementing policies and operating practices that enhance company competitiveness while advancing economic and social conditions in communities where it operates. In other words, it is about identifying and expanding the connection between society and economic progress (Porter and Kramer 2011). This all sounds interesting and (possibly) hopeful. Shared value is described as the right kind of profits, thus providing a chance for business to earn back society's respect.

This chapter explores the topic of shared value in some detail to probe its underlying mechanisms. Fortunately, a recent report has appeared with Michael Porter as a co-author, entitled "Measuring Shared Value" (Porter, Hills, et al. n.d.), and it tries to describe how measurement of shared value could take place. In the new report the authors focus on a tool for measurement. It was believed that to drive shared value in practice, a measurement framework was needed that focused on the interaction between business and social results. Porter cautions that companies currently lack the data that would be required to optimize the results of shared value initiatives.

The starting point for a shared value initiative is a shared value strategy. This is not surprising, because Michael Porter is one of the foremost authorities on business strategy, and is the originator of the 5 forces approach to strategy. In the new report on shared value (Porter, Hills, et al. n.d.), he notes that measurement makes shared value tangible for investors, and three approaches to shared value are listed (repeated from the original 2011 paper that introduced the topic).

The first approach is reconceiving products and markets. The basic idea is to focus on revenue growth, market share, and profitability that arise from economic, social, or environmental benefits from new products and services. This is about figuring out ways that your products and services can serve a wider audience in your external environment to grow revenue and market share, while generating shared value in the process. The second approach is about redefining productivity in the value chain. This involves improvements in internal operations that improve cost, input access, quality, or productivity. It could include things like better resource utilization, investments in employees, and investments in supplier capabilities. The third approach is enabling cluster development, which focuses on improving the external environment through community investments, local suppliers, and local infrastructure.

Let's look at some ways that these ideas have been carried out in specific companies. Porter outlines a four-step process for implementation. The first is on the strategy side, to identify the social issues that the business would like to focus on. Here the business would look around its environment to find the key social issues that it might have an opportunity to address. The second step is to identify the business case that would generate both economic value for the company as well as social value for society at large. If a positive decision has been made to go ahead with the intervention, Step three is tracking progress. Step four is about measuring results, and adjusting the approach to make it better for the next round.

In our first example, Coca Cola implemented a shared value initiative in Brazil. First, they identified the social issue to be unemployed youth. Even though the education system did a good job of educating the youth, many were unable to find employment. Coca Cola decided to invest in training the youth in entrepreneurial and retail activities. Under the program, the youth received two months of intensive training in running a retail shop, business development, and entrepreneurship. Then they were paired with a local retailer, presumably one that was selling Coca Cola products. In this effort, they were looking to address the lower middle class segment.

Over several years, Coca Cola developed more than 135 collectives, each with about 500 students. In 2012, the most recent year discussed, about 170 collectives were active. The basic idea was to use youth job placement to improve youth self-esteem, as well as increase company sales and brand connection. The initiative was expected to turn a profit within two years. Originally, the focus was on the technical skills of the youth, but it was found that some had low self-esteem, so more emphasis was added on soft skills, including leadership and presence as a retailer/ entrepreneur. An NGO partner was also enlisted in the endeavor, where several million dollars were invested to improve management and leadership of the NGO, and to help it find sustainable sources of outside funding. Overall, the effort was viewed as a successful implementation of shared value.

Another example of the shared value approach comes from Novo Nordisk, the diabetes control company that serves a large portion of the world market for insulin. The problem they identified was that urban populations in China were increasingly prone to diabetes. In 2010, for instance, 40 million cases of Type II diabetes were reported in China, and the number was expected to double within 15 years (by 2025). The basic intervention strategy involved improvement of the government healthcare system, including diabetes care in China. The program envisaged improved training for physicians, educational outreach for potential patients, and investments in the local production of insulin.

Novo Nordisk began its program two decades ago, so they have been at it for a while. It was found that the company could improve its bottom line financial results while improving the lives of millions of Chinese at the same time. Reported activities included a diabetes screening tour of 100 cities, where 60,000 patients were screened for diabetes, and free education sessions were offered for physicians. As a result of the program, the company demonstrated considerable improvement in diabetes control, and the company's market share went up from 40% to 63% in China, the world's second largest insulin market.

Another example of a shared value initiative is Intel's education transformation strategy. The problem that the company identified was improving student outcomes and sales of classroom technology. The basic idea was to integrate technology into a holistic training philosophy for IT education. In targeted schools, only 5% of students had access to a personal computer or to the internet at school, per their data, and teachers lacked professional development and curricula assessment approaches to integrate technology into the classroom. Intel initiated a program called Intel Teach, which trained 13 million teachers worldwide. They partnered with several developing countries to provide a one-stop solution for teaching and providing technology in the classroom. As they investigated how well the initiative worked out, they monitored several variables, such things as the ruggedness of the equipment (including its water resistance, its battery life), and how well the teachers and students engaged with it. A virtuous cycle emerged from this effort, and additional sales were a result. Other benefits included a market share increase for Intel, and improved educational outcomes for the students and their schools.

A shared value initiative was also undertaken by Nestle, which was having trouble getting high quality raw materials for its agricultural products. It decided to train and assist small holder farmers in rural areas of India, as follow-on to an activity that the company began in 1961, when Nestle started its first milk district. The program concentrated on giving advice to 110,000 farmers, and providing veterinary services for their animals. In Rajasthan alone, the program enrolled 8,000 farmers.

Given these examples, how does shared value differ and overlap with existing practices? For starters, there seems to be a good deal of difficulty in carrying out the measurement side of things. There are existing social performance management practices that cover sustainability and social and economic value, as well as development impact, reputation, and compliance. Shared value measurement has focused on measuring how social outcomes directly drive tangible business value creation. Current management practices seem to be insufficient to inform shared value strategies, so it is difficult to find the connection between business value and social value that promises to shift the fundamental connection between business and social progress.

Investors remain skeptical about the connection between a company's performance on social issues and the creation of economic value. The evidence is often called into question, especially the question of causality. Shared value measurement looks at the economic value accrued to the business from improving social outcomes without estimating the value of the social change. Whether the shared value initiative lives up to its billing seems to be problematic. The way it is conceptualized right now, shared value focuses on the interface between how business and nonprofit organizations could work together in joint initiatives, involving joint objectives and goals and to which they each contribute added value. The aim is to generate economic value and social value beyond that which would be generated in a strictly instrumental supply chain linking firms, suppliers, and buyers (Brandenburger and Stuart 1996).

Steve Denning, writing in *Forbes*, discusses whether shared value reinvents capitalism (S. Denning 2011b). He sees aspects to it that are welcome, because it expands the traditional view of the firm. While a firm is often focused on making money for itself from its customers without regard to society's interests, shared value expands that view of the world. Shared value proposes that what is good for society can also be good for business, because it posits that business has missed some profit opportunities that would benefit society. It encourages participants to look broadly at how non-customers could be served, or perhaps look to areas of the value chain where things like environmental costs, energy use, or packaging costs could be reduced — which would both save money for the firm and benefit society.

What shared value does not do, per Denning, is that it doesn't abandon conventional financial analysis for evaluating investments, so the new opportunities that are found are subjected to return-on-investment (ROI) analysis. Denning's point is that since these are traditional forms of analysis, they are unable to shield firms from the types of disruptive innovation that has been crippling in the past.

Shared value is about pursuing profit in new ways, but it is still about pursuing profit. In a sense, it is a form of traditional management. It uses the goal model, for instance, for effectiveness – where an organization is effective to the extent that it achieves its goals, and those goals are focused on the profit motive. The entire narrative about capitalism doesn't change a lot with just the addition of shared value. Shared value initiatives still follow the old ways, but they look for opportunities to serve those that have not been served, using new and different approaches that are good for both society and business.

In the alternative approach advocated in this book, Management by Positive Organizational Effectiveness (M+OE) provides a framework where the goal of every organization is the same: to be effective within its environment, while strengthening the whole (the common good). The advantage of M+OE (and the OFM) compared to the goal model is that progress is measured against an objective reality, that is, how effective an organization's offerings are within its environment, and whether they are improving the environment overall, rather than degrading it. Shared value initiatives could be viewed as a subset of possibilities available under M+OE, but are likely to offer only a partial view of what needs to be explored in the future. Shared value is not likely to reinvent capitalism, despite its early claims, but it is an attempt to move in the right direction none the less.

CHAPTER 10

THE PURPOSE-DRIVEN ORGANIZATION

You may have heard of the purpose-driven organization. The basic idea seems to go back to a book by Rick Warren, *The Purpose-Driven Church* (1995). According to Warren, the purpose-driven church was originally designed to remove the barriers that were keeping churches from growing. "God wants churches to grow," says Warren. In an online video, he points out that the job of the church is to transform people from an initial "come and see" attitude (when they first join the church), to an attitude where they are willing to "come and die" (i.e., dying to self, using Christ's example). This is the high calling of service to humanity that is encouraged by the purpose-driven church.

In 2006, author Nikos Mourkogiannis described the purpose-driven company as a company driven to be great. "A great company is one that embodies a purpose in such a way that its quality of action is high," he wrote. He viewed it as a company that "not only sustains itself, but it provides continuing evidence of the value of its existence" (Mourkogiannis 2006).

By 2013-2014, the purpose-driven company idea had emerged in the mainstream media. For instance, author Sherry Hakimi writes in *Fast Company* that purpose-driven companies are often more successful (Hakimi 2015). While it's hard to survive in today's economy, she writes, the companies that figure it out have something in common — the pursuit of purpose alongside the pursuit of profit. Purpose mobilizes people in a way that pursuing profits alone does not. An organization without purpose *manages* people and resources, while an organization with purpose *mobilizes* people and resources. Purpose is thus a key ingredient for a strong, sustainable, and scalable organizational culture. It is an unseen, yet ever-present element that drives an organization forward.

One example given in the *Fast Company* article is a household goods company called Seventh Generation. They manufacture consumer products like dish soap, fabric softener, and toilet paper; but the company's products are authentically imbued with a higher purpose — to inspire a consumer revolution that nurtures the health of the next 7 generations. This is an idea that combines purpose with profits, essentially to have a 'vision' plus 'values statement' that mobilizes employees and lifts their spirits toward a higher goal. What they are looking for in purpose is a clear and comprehensive narrative that knits an organization's mission, vision, and values together and offers a sense of purpose. In its absence, it is believed, a company's leadership is likely to have greater difficulty in motivating employees and putting the company on the course to success. With purpose, however, a company has the potential to create positive value that is far greater than the sum of its parts.

A *Forbes* article profiled the world's top purpose-driven organizations that sought to use business as a force for good (Skoll World Forum 2013). They described the results of a study that looked at 500 companies. These were companies where the objective wasn't to maximize profit, but rather to maximize benefit to people and the planet. What wasn't clear, they said, was how to keep score.

Normally we think of nonprofits as being purpose-driven, but there is a significant movement toward casting for-profit organizations as purpose driven as well. Examples that were given in the *Forbes* article include Whole Foods, IDEO, Google, and Zappos (Skoll World Forum 2013). Author Anne Loehr writes in the *Huffington Post* that "finding purpose at work doesn't mean you have to work in the rainforests of the Amazon protecting endangered wildlife" (Loehr 2015). Purpose can be found in any position, since it is about how you approach a job, rather than the nature of the job itself. Purpose offers a new employee value proposition that relates to personal growth, relationships, and impact in the world. A purpose-driven company values its employees and its environment in holistic ways, and tries to make its values tangible by stating them openly and visibly. In doing so, it seeks to attract new employees, as well as retain existing employees for the long term.

The editors of the *Academy of Management Journal* have noted that trust in business is improving from its low point in 2009, but remains dishearteningly low (AMJ editors 2014). They cited surveys reporting that only one in four members of the public trust business leaders to correct issues when necessary, and only one in five trusts business to tell the truth, and to make ethical and moral decisions. The conduct of business was said to often consume trust rather than create it, while trust successfully embodied in a brand often reflected a reputation from the past. General discussions about capitalism typically support the view that a corporation is an economic agent, a position often blamed on business schools and sustained by regulations prescribing corporate and managerial behavior.

The AMJ editors suggest that the answer lies, fundamentally, in redefining organizations as purposeful, and allowing purpose to define an expanded scope for business activity. The AMJ calls for greater attention to the rediscovery of purpose, by identifying themes that link purpose to the larger values that promote society's wellbeing.

Purpose can provide an overarching framework, AMJ believes, and open new opportunities for the role of business in society. For them, business and society are interdependent; one cannot flourish without the other. Focusing on purpose creates a challenge for all businesses in terms of promoting the common good, or genuinely aiming to provide products and services that benefit society. This requires paying attention to the least of society, although every decision of every business cannot benefit all. The issue is more about how business should think about its impact, both positive and negative, particularly its effects on those with the smallest voices. Serving the common good mandates not only the pursuit of individual goals, but participation in joint or common initiatives that benefit the whole. The AMJ editors listed six values that they believed could potentially help organizations achieve purpose (AMJ editors 2014, 1229). In summary, AMJ noted an urgent need to reframe how we understand the purpose of business in society (AMJ editors 2014, 1233).

One way that companies have found to officially incorporate purpose-driven missions in their corporate by-laws is by legally incorporating as a benefit corporation. In a benefit corporation, a company's core social and environmental values are elevated to the status of law. This helps to protect directors over the long term, and to manage the expectations of shareholders, who may have a spectrum of opinions about the role of the company's social and environmental mission (Honeyman 2014).

This chapter has explored the background of the purpose-driven organization, and the purpose-driven company. It seems to me, the problem with the purpose-driven organization is that there is no way to determine whether the right purpose has been selected. The purpose-driven organization has the same problem that other management frameworks have, it uses the goal model for effectiveness (an organization is effective to the extent that it achieves its goal). Goals are not created equal, however, and it is difficult to know whether progress is being assessed against an objective reality that can be tied to organizational effectiveness.

In contrast to the purpose-driven organization, Management by Positive Organizational Effectiveness (M+OE) provides a framework where the goal (or purpose) of every organization is the same: to be effective within its environment, while strengthening the whole (the common good). As mentioned in the previous chapter, the advantage of M+OE (and the OFM) compared to the goal model is that progress is measured against an objective reality, that is, how effective an organization's offerings are within its environment, and whether they are improving the environment overall, rather than degrading it.

A view was expressed at the beginning of this chapter that the purpose-driven company was more successful, and that may be the case when compared to organizations that are not purpose driven. The purpose-driven company seeks not only to sustain itself, but to supply evidence of the value of its existence on a regular basis. When employees aspire to align with a larger purpose, they acknowledge a desire that we all have to connect with a higher good. Through the 3-phase process outlined in this book, M+OE seeks to satisfy this desire in a comprehensive and direct manner.

CHAPTER 11

ORGANIZATIONS MAY SAVE
THE PLANET, OR NOT

I recently listened to a podcast episode from Radio Lab entitled "Cellmates" (Radio Lab Podcast 2016). It told a strange story that started some 4 billion years ago, with single-celled organisms floating in a primordial sea. It put forth a theory about how life on Earth emerged from tiny bags of chemicals floating in this sea, to the vast menagerie of creatures that came after. The theory is based on a book entitled *The Vital Question*, by Nick Lane (2015).

A key event in the story was said to have occurred about 2 billion years ago, when two types of single-celled organisms merged, seemingly by accident (one gaining internal hardware and software from the other) to make possible the large multi-celled organisms that came later. Present-day mitochondria within all our cells provide the evidence that this early merger took place. The mind-blowing implication is that all multi-celled organizations have come from this merger (according to the theory), as part of the evolutionary sequence. Much later, early human-like creatures appear on the scene, use fire to cook their food, and develop big brains. The rest, as they say, is history. So far, only humans have been found to have a self-awareness of who they are, and are able to question where they have come from.

Inspired by the story, it struck me that organizations can be thought of as the next step in this lineage if we take a macro view. Consider what organizations represent: within them, humans are encased within a super-organism (if only during part of their day), gain an energy source, band together with other like-minded individuals to find purpose and meaning, and accomplish things together that they could not do on their own. A successful organization is a form of super-organism, often with access to considerable power and resources over time. Chester Barnard (1938) noted the relationship between humanity's ability to organize and our species' evolution, identifying organizations as the most advanced means to improve cooperation beyond current limits, the furthest step in human evolution, and a magnificent human achievement (Solari 2016). It is no wonder that organizations large and small dominate the world around us, and that we find them so indispensable.

Now some 150 years after the first tiers of middle management appeared in US railroads, we are under the spell of managerial capitalism (collectively, managers are in control of the economy, rather than the free market), and firms have grown to very large size, serving domestic and international markets. Yet an organization can be viewed as good or bad for our world, depending upon which values are expressed in its processes. The 'negative' category embody negative values (think Enron and other corporations disgraced by scandal, terrorist organizations such as ISIL and al Qaeda, and the seemingly ever-present drug cartels). These are types of organizations that do not embody, in one way or another, positive human values (e.g., honesty, respect for the law, peacefulness, environmental conservation, etc.). Even where so-called 'positive' organizations operate, the world as we know it may be threatened by negative externalities that are the byproduct of global economic activity (e.g., Global Warming, sea level rise, depletion of scarce resources, etc.) when organizations do not build up the whole. What to do?

Well, where organizations create such problems, only organizations can solve them. Organizations will save the planet, or not. Most of us expect to be part of the solution rather than part of the problem. Just as DNA provided a biological code to replicate and evolve organisms from the distant past to the present, new management theory and practice is needed to provide a template for the coming age (one of organizational effectiveness?). To stabilize the planet, we need organizations that search for and demonstrate positive, win-win-win results chains that are effective, then help replicate them elsewhere through others. In short, we need to serve our environment to be rewarded in return — to build up the whole rather than degrade it. We still live on one little blue dot in the vast darkness of space.

What leads me to believe that organizations can save the planet? It is the outcome-focused model for OE, which gives rise to Management by Positive Organizational Effectiveness (M+OE). Importantly, it can be applied to all types of organizations. It can also be applied when loose coalitions of organizations work together toward a common purpose (e.g., to save the world). M+OE provides a way to achieve great things.

By now we have explored all the threads to the story of why we need to enter a new age (first noted in the Prologue). One thread described the prevalence of 'efficiency-ism,' which holds organizations back from realizing their true potential. Another thread described the widespread dissatisfaction with what capitalism has now become. Still another outlined the difficult situation that society finds itself in on multiple fronts, with limited options, and no clear path forward. We have also described other voices that have tried, but have not found a clear way ahead.

We have now completed Part II of the book. It has been a significant journey, and we have come far. The gate of a new age is in front of us, and we are prepared to enter — the Age of Organizational Effectiveness (in Part III of the book).

PART III

ENTERING THE AGE OF
ORGANIZATIONAL EFFECTIVENESS

Part III of the book consists of the final 5 chapters (Chapters 12-16). It delivers you into the Age of Organizational Effectiveness, and describes the style of management found there -- termed Management by Positive Organizational Effectiveness (M+OE).

Chapter 12 encourages you to "think different" in order to enter the new age.

Chapter 13 outlines the process for testing and discovering effectiveness within your environment.

Chapter 14 gives examples of companies that exhibit positive organizational effectiveness now.

Chapter 15 considers how a new style of management can program the organization for effectiveness, including both manual work and knowledge work.

Chapter 16, "Become Truly Great," concludes the series. Great organizations occupy a niche within their environment and their actions serve to strengthen the whole ecosystem, rather than weaken it.

In summary, Part III completes the 3 phase M+OE process that was initiated earlier with "Be Virtuous" (Chapter 5); now find "Discover Effectiveness" (Chapter 13) and "Become Truly Great" (Chapter 16) in this, the final section of the book.

CHAPTER 12

"THINK DIFFERENT"
ABOUT EFFECTIVENESS

In 1997, Apple began an ad campaign called "think different," which featured billboards with large pictures of notably famous people like Albert Einstein, Thomas Edison, Amelia Earhart and others alongside the Apple logo and an ad slogan that said, "think different." Apple wanted to associate its brand with greatness. The implication was that by purchasing an Apple product the customer was beginning to think different, and was embarking upon a path that could lead to great things. The long-lived ad campaign proved to be an enormous commercial success for Apple, and is credited with restoring its reputation after an 11-year period in which Steve Jobs had been absent from the firm (Hormby 2013).

When it comes to organizational effectiveness, few organizations think different. The most common way to think about effectiveness is by using the goal model. There are few organizations that do not use it in some way. In this model, an organization is effective to the extent that it achieves its goals and objectives. Management by objectives, first popularized by Peter Drucker in 1954, is derived from the goal model (Drucker [1954/1982] 1993). Today's computer-based scorecards, dashboards, and indicator monitoring systems that organizations have adopted widely, take the idea to the next level. It's the goal model on steroids; but the goal model does not reliably improve effectiveness.

Why? Even advocates of the goal model admit that not all goals are created equal, and it is hard to argue that all goals relate to organizational effectiveness. Often, goal setters are simply admonished to set clear goals, with the emphasis on clarity. Another framework for goal setting calls for SMART goals (Specific, Measurable, Attainable, Relevant, and Timely). But it is not sufficient to set goals based on so-called SMART criteria, as these criteria do not ensure effectiveness.

Let's think about why we set organizational goals in the first place. In the common view, goals offer people within an organization clarity of purpose. The idea is that with a "big hairy, audacious goal," or some variation thereof, even if it's not fully achieved, the organization will be driven toward significant achievement. It's sort of like playing a video game, where you try to beat your old score, or the score of a competing team, by trying to do better this time. It's about tapping into our seemingly inbuilt drive for competitiveness. But tapping into the competitiveness of its employees may not improve the effectiveness of the organization. Using the goal model, an organization can easily fall prey to the tyranny of efficiencyism (discussed in Chapter 1) by focusing on the wrong goals.

There is, I believe, a more meaningful way to think about effectiveness and goal setting: the outcome-focused model, or OFM (Chapter 7). Under the OFM, goals can be divided into four levels or categories, based on their standing within a results hierarchy. The four levels are inputs, outputs, outcomes, and impacts (refer back to Figure 7.2). The first two (inputs and outputs) are on the supply side and are within the control of the organization itself. Organizations convert inputs into activities that produce outputs. Outputs become offerings to the external environment (in the form of products and services, or projects and programs). The remaining two (outcomes and impacts) are on the demand side and are outside the control of the organization. Why does this matter? It is because, under the OFM, an organization is effective to the extent that it achieves its expected external outcomes. The OFM does not motivate an organization's employees to be competitive, but rather tries to motivate demand-side actors to adopt and use its offerings. This is a more useful and meaningful way to think about effectiveness.

When we refer to an outcome in the OFM, we do not mean a final result such as is assumed in the goal model. Rather, an outcome within the OFM is an effect caused by an antecedent event. While outputs are produced by the organization in the form of its offerings, it is demand-side actors that must decide if an organization's offerings are attractive enough to compel them to exhibit the behaviors of uptake, adoption or use. When such behaviors do occur, they can be observed in the real world, and supply the "objective referent" that has been missing in models of organizational effectiveness thus far.

You may recall that the US Army, back in 2001, changed its ad campaign and slogan, from the old slogan ("Be all you can be") to the new slogan "Army of One." In the new ad campaign (Dao 2001), each soldier was to think of himself or herself as an army of one. We could envisage a similar approach under the OFM. Since the goal of every organization is to be effective within its environment, every employee is empowered to wake up each day and reinterpret what it means to "serve your environment" anew. It is clear, however, that "serve your environment and be rewarded in return" is not about extracting as much profit as possible from every customer. It's about serving every customer and being sure that they receive the value that they are expecting. Potentially, this could create a very flat organization. Do you really need a highly-incentivized C-suite and a well-paid Board? Perhaps not. The OFM gives clarity of purpose to every level of the organization. In fact, it could make sense to take a portion of the compensation that is being paid to the C-suite and the Board, and redistribute it to front-line teams.

Will you "think different" to make your organization effective? You don't have to buy Apple products to create a great organization. Instead, adoption of Management by Positive Organizational Effectiveness (M+OE) would be a good start. In the next chapter, we explore what it takes to discover effectiveness under M+OE. Arguably, this is what "think different" is all about.

CHAPTER 13

DISCOVER EFFECTIVENESS (PHASE 2 OF M+OE)

An effective organization is focused on outcomes

An often-quoted view among organizational consultants and practitioners is that "efficiency is about doing things right, while effectiveness is about doing the right things" (Drucker 1966). Peter Drucker meant this statement to refer to the effectiveness of executives, not their organizations. When it comes to organizations, efficiency experts proudly declare that efficiency is the domain of doing the right things right the first time and every time. Effectiveness, on the other hand (as we have seen in Chapter 7), is something entirely different. It is *not about doing anything* within the organization. It is about achieving something outside of it.

Under the outcome-focused model (OFM), the goal of every organization is the same, that is, to be effective within its environment. Achievement of this goal encourages an outcome-focused strategy, where the organization verifies its effectiveness and calibrates its management initiatives based on behavioral responses from key external stakeholders to one or more of its offerings. It may appear tautological that the OFM deems organizations effective to the extent that they achieve desired effects; however, tautology is not present because results chain hypotheses can fail.

The OFM focuses the attention of the organization on its external interface and it is encouraged to be in-tune with the immediate and future needs of its environment. Upstream quality standards direct the attention of organizational units, including management and staff, to the need for early testing and validation of internal initiatives via favorable demand-side responses. The focus on expected external outcomes (EEO behaviors) changes the way that outputs are designed and delivered because internal actors come to realize that *outputs* are waste without the achievement of expected *outcomes*.

This approach should not be reduced to 'getting close' to the customer through focus groups or satisfaction surveys, although these may help. What users say is not necessarily what they do. Rather, it is about *observing* customer and end-user behaviors (i.e., EEOs) to verify results chain effectiveness. It is also about understanding end-user reality in sufficient detail to verify that they are capturing a high level of expected economic, social, and/or other benefits for themselves at an attractive cost (in both financial and non-financial terms).

Peter Drucker once observed that "the first thing to do to make sure that a program will not have results is to have a lofty objective – 'health care' for instance or 'to aid the disadvantaged'" (Drucker 1999b, 36). Within the OFM, these are inappropriate objective statements, more akin to a description of what the program does rather than a proper statement of what the program is expected to accomplish within its environment. It confuses means (activities and their supply-side outputs) with ends (expected demand-side outcomes and impacts).

Unfortunately, too many organizations are driven by inappropriate output-level objectives rather than outcome-level objectives, focusing their attention on efficiency rather than effectiveness. This can promote false-positive indicators of effectiveness where true effectiveness may not exist. An outcome-focused organization would avoid these problems by focusing its objectives on outcome-level results (EEOs), that is, on the behavior of actors outside the direct control of the organization who are expected to adopt and use its offerings. For example, an NGO's objective "to aid the disadvantaged" (an activity statement posing as an objective) would be transformed into an outcome-level objective such as "members of the disadvantaged target group utilize [the offered services] for [the purposes intended]." The former could be seen as a supply-driven and never-ending mandate that would require larger budgets year after year, while the achievement of the latter would require a real demand-side response via a focused strategy and a verified results chain to signify effectiveness. There is an added advantage in the latter approach that the services can be discontinued if their utilization by the target group diminishes over time (signifying decreased effectiveness).

In a police department, objective statements such as "to maintain law and order" or "to prevent crime" (activity-level statements vaguely indicating the type of work being undertaken on the supply side by the department) would be replaced with outcome-level statements focused on demand-side behavioral change, such as "to reduce the incidence of criminal behavior [during the holiday period]." This is an objective that can be taken seriously due to its sharp focus on demand-side results, and its time-bounded nature. In addition to outcome-focused objectives, the OFM requires outcome-focused indicators to quantify it targets, as discussed below.

There is a belief in some circles that "you don't get what you want, you get what you measure" (Bush Administration 2008). Yet despite the down-to-earth wisdom of this idea when applied appropriately, it remains very important to carefully select what will be measured. If achieving organizational effectiveness were simply about measuring a set of key performance indicators (KPIs), then most organizations would be performing very well today. Unfortunately, not all KPIs are created equal, and measurement alone does not verify causal linkages. Organizations often miss the point that before investing in a measurement initiative, strategies need to be well crafted, objectives and associated indicators properly set (at the outcome level), and one or more results chains identified and validated. Only then can a specific KPI be relied upon to provide a short-hand measure of effectiveness.

Quality standards serve to integrate efficiency with effectiveness in the OFM

It was mentioned earlier (Chapter 7) that some traditions from quality management have been adopted within the OFM. These often come in the form of standards, which serve to build quality into internal processes at their upstream initiation in an attempt to eliminate downstream waste and rework (i.e., by eliminating defects). When designing an effective organization — either from the start or by recasting an existing organization — quality criteria are also helpful in selecting initiatives to undertake and those to avoid. Based on the OFM, an effective organization implements initiatives that:

1. are consistent with its mission/vision and grow out of its core competencies and positive values;
2. offer real economic, social, or other benefits to actors within the environment;
3. have been tested (as appropriate) on their ability to bring about specific and worthwhile EEOs among customers or other key stakeholder groups;
4. embody a focused and realistic strategy;
5. meet or exceed standards for quality that conform to customer, end user, and internal stakeholder expectations (or requirements); and
6. can be expected to document and achieve useful results (planned outputs, expected outcomes and longer-term impacts) within the time frame and resources allocated.

Can effectiveness be compared across organizations?

Connolly, Conlon, and Deutsch (1980, 216) found the question "Is General Motors more or less effective than HEW?" to be of the same order as "Is an elephant more or less effective than a giraffe?" These are classic comparisons of apples to oranges. The OFM would give the same finding, largely because each organization is trying to do something different, and effectiveness is judged only on what an organization is trying to do (its intentions) through its offerings. The mix of offerings will be different for each organization, even when some offerings duplicate or compete with those of another organization. In addition, each organization lives in and serves an environment of its choosing (although some aspects are not under its control). Thus, it makes little sense to compare the overall effectiveness of one organization to another; however, the effectiveness of competing offerings could be compared between organizations in some cases. It is important to note, that the effectiveness of an organization is dynamic, and it makes sense to track OE longitudinally (a view shared by Aldrich (1979), as well as Hannan and Freeman (1989)) to provide timely evidence on which to base management action.

Organizational effectiveness (OE) as the dependent variable of choice

It could be argued that the advent of the OFM enables OE to reclaim its former position as the ultimate dependent variable for organizational research (described by Cameron & Whetten (1983, 2). As the goal of every organization, effectiveness could also become the *summum bonum* of organizational performance once again.

The OFM is expected to be useful in determining the effectiveness of an organization as a whole, its component parts (i.e., organizational units, when externally focused), or externally-focused projects and programs of an organization (or groups of organizations). Indications are that the OFM is applicable to organizations of all types (business, government, or nonprofit), large or small (Fortune 100, or less than 100 employees), without known constraints.

The Benefits of Organizational Effectiveness

It was mentioned previously (Chapter 7) that effectiveness is about the conversion of the supply-side intentions of an organization into the demand-side behaviors of uptake, adoption or use of its offering. So, let's say that the organization (on the supply side) is converting inputs, to activities, to outputs, all within the control of the organization (Figure 7.2). The outputs are then offered to the external environment, and actors in the environment are expected to recognize the value of those offering and decide to use them, purchase them, or in other ways take advantage of their benefits. Chapter 7 formulated a hierarchy of benefits with respect to exchanges between the organization and its environment (Figure 7.3): from the lower to higher, financial & economic, social & psychological, and environmental & spiritual.

If I am a customer, standing at the supply/demand interface, a quick calculation goes through my head: are the benefits of this transaction worth the costs that I will pay. If I am paying money for a product that the organization is offering, that is a financial flow to the organization. It goes into their bank account. In return, I'm getting an economic benefit, because I use the product over time. In a sense, I am making a bet that the product is going to last a long time, and that I am going to receive more in terms of economic benefits by using it than I paid in financial costs. On the transaction level, it's a simple exchange of financial benefits for economic benefits. There may be other benefits that I receive as a consumer, however, including social benefits, psychological benefits, and even environmental benefits.

Let's explore a real-world example. Suppose I want to buy a riding lawnmower. Now, a riding lawnmower is a sizable purchase. I might spend $1,000-$3,000, depending upon the model that I purchase. But how should I think about the transaction? There are several types of benefits that are being exchanged in this kind of transaction: financial, economic, social, and psychological benefits are probably the most prominent.

Exactly how does that work? I'm going to be handing over my cash, or my credit card. So, my payment is a financial benefit that goes to the retailer (some of which makes its way back to the manufacturer, while the retailer keeps the rest). That's the financial benefit stream. But I get economic benefits in return. As I hand over my cash, I'm expecting that the benefits that I will receive from using the lawn mower over time will be greater than the cost that I have to pay.

If I hire someone to mow the lawn instead of buying a lawn mower, I may spend $30 a week to get the job done. In paying $30 a week, times four weeks a month, times 9 months a year (not counting winter), that's $1,080 a year in financial cost that I could spend hiring someone to mow the lawn. But, if I go to the store and buy a riding mower for $1,500, I can use it for several years to mow the lawn myself. Even if gasoline and maintenance is $200 per year, the lawn mower would pay for itself (in terms of economic return) in about 1.5 years, compared to my out of pocket costs if I hired someone to do the job.

But that's not all, because there are likely to be social and psychological benefits associated with this do-it-yourself activity (depending upon the social setting). As I am mowing my lawn, I could receive social benefits through positive interactions with my neighbors, as they come to know me as a useful and productive member of the community. I may also accrue psychological benefits for myself as I'm doing this activity, if I gain in self-esteem. Environmental benefits (serving the common good) may also come into play as I help create a better neighborhood in which to live. So, the reason why somebody might be motivated to buy a lawn mower may have several dimensions. It's not only about the money (financial payment to the retailer in exchange for the economic benefits that I derive from using the asset over time). It is also about the other benefits that I can expect to receive (e.g., social, psychological, and environmental) that encourage and motivate me to make the purchase.

This may not be news to retailers, who typically try to suggest to the consumer the range of benefits that he/she would receive from the purchase. Their advertising copy often comes complete with pictures of the lawnmower being used in an attractive neighborhood, with smiling neighbors and flowering plants. You get the idea.

Essentially, all benefits that accrue to the organization come because of its effectiveness, or perceptions of effectiveness (because that's how it has been defined in the OFM). Whenever a business sells something, the exchange that takes place across the interface is evidence of current effectiveness. There are many alternative ways that the consumer could spend his/her money: by buying a different kind of product, by going to a variety of retailers on the web, or by visiting other brick-and-mortar shops. There are a high number of alternatives available to the consumer these days. The fact that customers are, in fact, purchasing from a given organization is evidence of its effectiveness within the marketplace. So, as the organization exists within its environment, the favorable behavior of the customer is direct evidence of effectiveness (i.e., actual interchanges across the interface). We can go out and observe those behaviors. When these behaviors can be induced in an intentional manner (largely at will) by the organization, the secret to effectiveness is within hand.

It may be useful here to review the results chain mentioned in an earlier chapter (see Figure 7.2). It begins with the inputs, which are converted into activities, which produce outputs (all on the supply side). The results chain then tries to achieve outcomes in the external environment, then cumulative impacts further in the future. It's the conversion of outputs to outcomes that verifies effectiveness, and the strength of that flow and that exchange is what keeps a business alive — because it's gaining financial income in exchange for what it's offering through its products and services.

If the organization is a nonprofit, the calculation is a bit different, because the donors that are supporting the nonprofit are not the direct users of the services. The donors are providing financial support to the nonprofit based on the perception of effectiveness, and the evidence of effectiveness is associated with the uptake, adoption, or use of the programs that the nonprofit is offering the actual users. Users may fall into a variety of different categories. If this is a youth organization, the nonprofit may be trying to influence the behavior of the youth. A problem might be identified that the youth are wasting their time hanging out on street corners and getting into mischief, for instance (the situation before the intervention). Afterwards, program effectiveness may envisage the youth pursuing careers because of some of the activities, the training, and connections and other benefits offered by the nonprofit. If the nonprofit is successful in involving the youth, getting the youth to participate – that uptake, adoption, or use of the program verifies the effectiveness of the results chain (depending upon the intervention logic). The donors, on the other hand, are supplying inputs due to the perceived effectiveness of the program. So, documentation of the outcomes needs to occur, and nonprofits are under a good deal of pressure these days to show that they are effective (in order to receive additional funding from their sources).

What we have tried to demonstrate is that the way in which effectiveness is defined in the OFM has very practical implications for management practice. One of the new ways to manage an organization made possible by the OFM is to monitor effectiveness daily, and that means observing demand-side responses at the interface between the organization and its environment. Of particular interest are the interchanges in which outputs are being converted to outcomes. EEO monitoring may be possible in real time on the web for some types of transactions. Businesses have run experiments with Google ads, for instance, offering products at different times, or with different discounts, to test the response from each in real time. Big data, combined with big computing power, can enable real-time outcome-fo-cused marketing experiments that open new avenues for performance monitoring.

In the government sector, the willingness of taxpayers to contribute their taxes is often based on their perceptions of government efficiency and effectiveness. We hear a lot of complaints these days from conservatives (and others) who imply that people do not like the way the government spends money, or the way the government is *perceived* to spend money. In any case, we can all agree that govern-ment needs to find better and more convincing ways to tell its story.

One way for government to tell its story in a better way is to break out each of its programs, services, and other initiatives (including projects), designing a results chain for each, then monitoring the demand-side response in real time (EEO behaviors). The advantage of this approach is that it allows the agency to monitor increases (or decreases) in effectiveness. This would allow agencies to begin to under-stand the causal factors underlying effectiveness (and to formulate approaches to serving the common good in better ways). We don't necessarily need smaller government or bigger government, but we do need effective government. M+OE (with the OFM) makes that possible.

This chapter has outlined ways that organizations can discover effectiveness by observing the types of benefit exchanges that take place at its boundary with the envi-ronment. I prefer to focus on 'observation' rather than 'measurement.' Observation includes measurement, if required, but it is not always necessary to measure, and it is often sufficient to observe. Managers need practical ways to understand whether an organization is effective or not, and this is what M+OE delivers.

CHAPTER 14

EXAMPLES OF POSITIVE ORGANIZATIONAL EFFECTIVENESS

In this chapter I want to provide examples of organizations that exhibit positive organizational effectiveness now. My examples are pulled solely from business, because they are the easiest to find, but I am sure that there are other organizations out there among nonprofits and government agencies that would be worthy of note. Let's look at a few organizations that appear to fit the model. My examples include Patagonia, Google (now under Alphabet), and Salesforce. These are not the only examples that could be found, or perhaps even the best examples that could be found, but they are examples that I found while researching this chapter. Inclusion here as an example is based primarily upon what an organization has said or stated in the media, with respect to their values and processes. While I have tried to verify my findings with other media sources, I have not visited these firms, nor have I corresponded with them. The examples are meant primarily to illustrate the principles of M+OE, and to indicate what we should be looking for in compiling such as list. The list, and its descriptive text, may appear a bit naive, due to the very brief treatment that can be given to each company in this setting, and the fact that I have limited knowledge of each. None the less, it represents a start.

For me, there are three indicators that comprise important markers of positive organizational effectiveness, and each corresponds to one of the three phases of M+OE: (1) be virtuous, (2) discover effectiveness, and (3) become truly great. First, we are looking for virtuous internal values and behaviors that focus on doing right by customers, employees, other stakeholders, and the common good (while avoiding scandal). The second indicator deals with whether the organization has discovered how to successfully create offerings that elicit the expected behaviors of uptake, adoption, or use by demand-side actors (e.g., customers), while building up the whole. Unfortunately, I do not have evidence that results chains have been designed and are being monitored for demand-side behaviors in the chosen companies, since I do not have first-hand knowledge of their processes. For the third indicator, I look for companies that are at least 5 years old that occupy of one or more niches that are vital to the functioning of the organization's chosen environment. I think of a niche in a biological sense, as the habitat in which an organization lives and its accompanying behavioral adaptations. Great organizations fill a niche within their environment, and are not often dislodged while they continue to do an outstanding job. Great organizations are also known for building up and improving their external environment, rather than degrading it.

Patagonia. First let's look at Patagonia in this way. I recently heard an interview with Yvon Chouinard, the founder of Patagonia. The company has been out front when it comes to being virtuous. All decisions are made with the idea that the company will be in business 100 years from now. The mission of the company is "to build the best product, cause no unnecessary harm, use business to inspire and implement solutions to the environmental crisis." Their clothes (designed for outdoor activities) come with a lifetime guarantee, and Patagonia is said to run the largest clothing repair business in North America, servicing not only their own garments, but those of other manufactures. Their employees benefit from on-site pre-K child care and education. Now 50-years old, Patagonia has an amazing story. The company is not focused on profit, but focused on delivering the best value for customers, while showing ways to improve the environment (Chouinard and Klein 2005/2016). Their chosen niche is equipping and clothing outdoor enthusiasts so that they can do their thing (e.g., climbing, kayaking, hiking, etc.) in the wild without harming the environment. They have served it well. The company is private, still 100% owned by the founder, but current sales are reported to be about $750 million a year. By all available markers, Patagonia exhibits the principles of positive organizational effectiveness now.

Google. While Google was restructured in 2015, and Alphabet is now the umbrella company which includes Google, we don't know enough about the other parts of the company to make much of a judgment. For now, let's use our framework to consider Google alone (which still includes Ads, Search, YouTube, Map, Apps, and Android), or some 90% of Alphabet's revenue (Rushe and Thielman 2015). Google focuses on the user above all else, because they feel that if they focus on the user, everything else will follow. Google has developed services that are mobile, and available in the cloud, to be accessed anywhere. Google-isms include, "you can make money without doing evil." "You know there's always more information out there." "The need for information crosses all borders." And finally, "great just isn't good enough."

Google is looking for the perfect search engine, and they serve their niche (web search) well. Some of their core values include: avoiding micromanagement, radical empowerment of employees, productivity and results, and helping employees realize their own career development goals. The culture of Google is said to be one of openness, general ethics, and corporate citizenship. Their purpose, as they state it, is "to organize the world's information and to make it universally accessible and useful."

Google has a lot of things going on (a taste of which can be found on the company blog), but in its totality the company seems to fulfill the three indicators mentioned earlier. They have virtuous internal values, they are getting strong uptake, adoption and use of their offerings, and they occupy a significant niche associated with search by making the world's information available to us all (while building up the common good). A steady stream of new innovations is being continually reported by the company. The reason for the reorganization was reportedly to instill a certain amount of discipline, financial and otherwise, on new initiatives, now receiving separate scrutiny under Alphabet (Google X, etc.). Google Ads continues to generate enormous amounts of cash, while many of the other initiatives are still in a development stage, and are doing the opposite (consuming cash). All in all, Google is another example of positive organizational effectiveness now.

Salesforce. Salesforce.com, a global cloud computing company, is my final example. Marc Benioff, the CEO, says that the business of business includes "improving the state of the world" (Benioff 2015), and he believes that the best way to create long-term shareholder value (without making it the goal) is to serve the interests of all stakeholders (customers, employees, partners, suppliers, citizens, governments, the environment and any other entity impacted by its operations).

Salesforce offers the #1 CRM (customer relationship management) system, offering cloud-based services that allow their customers to run aspects of their business on-line while gaining built-in improvements in productivity. Corporate values are very positive, and employees receive seven paid days a year to volunteer in nonprofits, as the company seeks to give back to its external environment. Salesforce. com was No. 23 on Fortune's list of the 100 best companies to work for in 2016 (although that was down somewhat from the year before). Salesforce represents another example of positive organizational effectiveness now.

Some companies that have been considered among the top performing organizations in the economy would not make my list, such as Amazon, Apple, and IBM. Amazon would not be among my examples of Positive Organizational Effectiveness now because of what has been reported as a difficult work environment (Kantor and Streitfeld 2015). Otherwise, Amazon seems to be obsessed with customers, is getting good uptake, adoption and use of its products and services, and is doing some good things, but concerns about the work environment for employees has prevented my use of Amazon as an example of positive organizational effectiveness now.

For me, Apple would not be a good example because their statement of purpose focuses on bringing great *products* to the planet. My feeling is that Apple is too focused on the supply side delivery of products (at least in their narrative), while Apple's real value seems to be in the pervasive customer experience, and their success in creating a line of products that seamlessly work together to create that customer experience (with great acceptance on the demand side). Customer experience is not reflected in their purpose statement, so I believe that they are not fully in tune with what would otherwise make them a great company.

IBM has not been included as an example because their C-suite has been highly incentivized to focus on shareholder value, which was mentioned in other chapters as leading to, and being a part of, efficiencyism. We need to move away from efficiencyism to enter the Age of Organizational Effectiveness. This would keep them off the list of organizations that serve as examples of positive organizational effectiveness now.

I hope the examples in this chapter have been useful, despite their brevity. They are meant to be illustrative of the criteria to be used in compiling examples of this type. The findings are based on the limited information available from media sources. More examples could be given, but I leave it up to the reader to consider their own candidates based on the limited discussion offered here.

CHAPTER 15

PROGRAMING THE ORGANIZATION FOR EFFECTIVENESS

Programming the work when the task is known

Programming manual work. Starting in the 1700s in England, the industrial revolution gradually enabled the application of machinery to the process of work and served to replace some of the more strenuous and repetitive tasks being carried out with human and animal power, through the substitution of machines. The steam engine was first used to pump water from mines in 1698. The period 1760-1840 in England saw the wide-spread replacement of hand production methods with production methods driven by machine. Steam engines (unlike water power) allowed the siting of factories close to towns where they were fed with fossil fuels (generally wood or coal). By the early-1800s, a textile factory using a 100 HP steam engine could do the work of 880 men. One documented example ran 50,000 spindles, employed 750 workers, and could produce 226 times more than it did before the introduction of steam. This impressive advance in productivity was partly due to the introduction of the French Argand lamp by 1810, which made round-the-clock shift work possible (Burke 1985, 192). All of this progress was in the service of efficiency.

I was recently re-reading Peter Drucker's book entitled *Management Challenges for the 21st Century*. According to Drucker, one of the main contributions of management in the 20th Century was to enable a 50-fold gain in the productivity of manual work (Drucker 1999a, 135). He attributed all the gain to the principles worked out by Frederick Winslow Taylor. Taylor invented what he called 'task analysis' or 'task management,' later called 'Scientific Management' in his book by the same name (Taylor [1911] 1998). Today we know these principles as a part of indus-trial engineering. Taylor started out as a manual laborer and then studied manual work, and according to Drucker, was the first person in history to both work as a laborer and then study manual work. That's surprising, considering that Greek and Roman writers and poets celebrated the work of the farmer and herdsman in song and in poetry, yet no one else seems to have gotten close to manual work and studied how to make it more productive until Taylor.

Taylor's intention was to ensure that the task of the worker was carried out in the most efficient manner. To bring this about he closely observed the work using time and motion studies. He wanted to apply the most suitable tools and methods to the work at hand, so that the time and motion involved in the task was minimized. When the worker (despite being unskilled) took advantage of the right tools to do the work, and moved in ways that were prescribed by one of Taylor's managers, a more pro-ductive way to work was created. Costs were lowered for the employer, and the wages of the worker could rise (a win-win, if done right).

Taylor found that whenever he studied the interaction of workers with their equipment, he found inefficiencies. In unskilled manual work, the required task is largely given; the main question is how best to do the work. After Taylor, an improved factory of the time built on ideas from the 1700s (specialization of labor, illustrated by Adam Smith's pin factory), with the further addition of Taylor's principles for the improvement of worker efficiency through specialization of equipment, and task management. Henry Ford's assembly line of 1913 was an application of Taylor's principles. The assembly line programed the manual worker because the sequence of assembly, and the time allocated for each step, was designed into the line (as the work moved to the worker).

Programming knowledge work. Another type of worker came to prominence in the mid-1800s, which Peter Drucker termed the 'knowledge worker." These workers take a body of knowledge and apply it to the work, and a large degree of cognition and discretion is required to do the work properly. We have come to know these workers as professionals — people like lawyers, doctors, engineers, and managers. Today, they generally have college degrees, although not always in earlier times. Since the body of knowledge that they apply in their chosen fields is not static, but is continually undergoing change, knowledge workers need to remain current in their field.

Let's look at a typical law office, in which the body of knowledge is the law. Lawyers go to law school, graduate, come out and take the bar exam, and then set up a law office and "practice law." In the court system, there are two sides to an argument, the prosecution and the defense, so the two sides are working against each other. The idea is to achieve justice under the law. Over the course of a career, the lawyer will gradually gain a reputation as he tries cases — winning some, losing others. For the lawyer, it's often about reputation, and how successful his case record is over time. The desired outcome is to win cases, but the first thing the lawyer cares about is being hired to work on a case, and that comes from reputation. To be productive, the experienced lawyer operates within a team that includes other professionals such as accounts, office administrators, and junior legal colleagues. The amount of compensation that the lawyer and his team receives typically grows over time as the reputation of the practice grows. The team operates within a professional practice (i.e., an organization), using processes designed by management to sequence the tasks associated with each case, and distribute them to the knowledge workers in a logical, timely, and efficient manner.

Let's turn to the doctor, and the doctor's office. The doctor is also applying a body of knowledge, which is gained from medical school. The doctor graduates, becomes a licensed physician, sets up a practice and begins attracting patients. It's her reputation, often spread by word of mouth, that normally attracts patients. Over time, her growing reputation, buoyed by the satisfaction of her patients, grows the practice and results in gradual increases in compensation to the doctor and her team. To be productive, the doctor operates within a team that includes other professionals, including administrators, accounts, nurses, and various other professionals that, working together, schedule the workflow. The team operates within a professional practice (i.e., an organization), using processes designed by management to sequence the tasks associated with each patient, and distribute them to the knowledge workers in a logical, timely, and efficient manner.

Take another case, in the inner-city school, where teachers try to educate their assigned students. Here, it is the school system that specifies the curriculum, the school facilities, the classroom dimensions. A team is assigned to the work, including administrative staff, a group of teachers, and even maintenance workers. There are several things that need to work properly to create a classroom environment in which students learn. The teacher is acting in a role, which has been specified in the system. Educational success depends on a lot of different things: how well the student was prepared from the previous year's studies, how willing the student is to learn, how conducive the home environment is to supporting the student's needs, and then how well the curriculum and the teaching process both perform. These factors may be highly variable from one classroom to the next. To be productive, the teacher operates within a team of colleagues that have different, but complementary, skills. The team operates within an educational institution (i.e., an organization), using processes designed by management (or administrators) to sequence the tasks associated with each student, or class of students, and distribute them to the knowledge workers in a logical, timely, and efficient manner. If students are not learning, it's not simply the teacher's fault. Rather, it is the systems' fault.

The knowledge workers we have discussed so far are from the traditional professions, e.g., doctor, lawyer, teacher. Here the work comes to the worker (and the task is largely known) – the patient to the doctor, the client to the lawyer, the student to the teacher. But, the same can be said for many other professionals, and office workers in general. Since the work comes to the worker, these knowledge workers become productive within a system that manages the scheduling of the work with the worker. It is a system that either they create themselves (if they are running their own practice) or someone else creates for them (as part of a larger organization). The basic ingredients of the system for knowledge worker productivity can be divided into two categories: 1) back office operations — which takes care of the administrative functions, such as personnel, accounting, budgeting, maintenance, facilities, etc., and 2) production operations — which organizes the internal production tasks in order to acquire the work (a customer), and then distribute the work to the individual knowledge workers in a logical, timely, and efficient manner. The knowledge worker remains in control of how the knowledge is applied to the work.

So far, what we have discussed has been largely about productivity (and efficiency), which is concerned with the rate of output (e.g., products and services) per unit of input. Taylor's "one best way" still comes to mind. But what about effectiveness? A third, and often missing part of the system is required to manage for effectiveness: a feedback loop from the external environment to verify that the outputs (i.e., offerings) being created are inducing their expected outcomes. It is about converting intention (to offer specific benefits to its environment through an offerings) into demand-side results (using EEO behaviors as markers for effectiveness).

This should be familiar by now. The effectiveness of a current offering is confirmed when EEO behaviors are observed at the supply/demand interface. If actors in the external environment (e.g., customers) are responding with the expected behaviors that signify uptake, adoption and use, then effectiveness is present. Interestingly, once an organization begins to focus on EEOs, it generally changes the character of the outputs being delivered. This is because once management begins to closely observe EEOs at the supply/demand interface, it will become apparent that the current offerings need to be improved in certain ways. Over time, a cumulative record of EEO behavior can chart the ups and downs of effectiveness under various conditions, and help explain the causal factors at work.

In the next section, we consider approaches that can be used to program knowledge work under a variety of circumstances when the task is unknown, as in adverse, complex, or unfamiliar environments.

Programming knowledge work when the task is unknown

There are many knowledge workers that do their work outside of an office, spending much of their time in the field. The work does not come to them, rather, they come to the work. Here productivity is more challenging, because scheduling the work with the worker is difficult, and moving around in the field is time consuming (and often nonproductive). Despite these challenges, the work can be very interesting and rewarding, and the environment becomes more predictable as the worker's (and the organization's) experience grows. This is the world of the adverse, complex, or unfamiliar environment. In this section, I mention a few examples of techniques that can be used to navigate this environment.

Positive deviance. Monique Sternin gave a TED Talk in 2013 that illustrates how to capitalize on positive deviance in the environment when the task is unknown. Positive deviance is essentially unexpected success beyond what is typically found within a group of peers. Monique tells a story about going to Vietnam to work on problems with child nutrition, particularly child malnutrition. When she arrived, she was met by government officials who were highly skeptical that she would be able to solve the problem of malnutrition. They said that they were only going to give her 6 months, and if there were no positive results within 6 months, they would not renew her visa.

She and her husband began the assignment by traveling to some of the pilot villages, where a high percentage of the children were malnourished. The first thing they decided to do was to weigh all the children, so they trained some volunteers for that purpose. Within four days or so they had the data on the children's weight. Then, they wondered whether there were some children who had normal weight in this environment, and were doing well under the adverse circumstances. All the children were from very poor families who were living in very poor villages, so they were curious as to whether they could find children that were doing fine despite their environment. Interestingly, they did find some children that had normal weight and we're doing fine. They visited the families of these normal children to ask what they were doing differently from the other families where the children were malnourished. They found that the children that were doing well, were being fed (on average) four times a day instead of 2 times a day, and the normal rice broth was being supplemented with shrimp and sweet potatoes that were available locally, although most people didn't eat them.

This finding represented positive deviance within the environment, and they took advantage of this knowledge by building a feeding program around it — thus testing the new practices among families of malnourished children. In rather short order, Monique was able to set up a program where the mothers of malnourished children were able to practice the behaviors that the families of normal weight children were practicing in the adverse environment. They allowed the mothers of malnourished children to practice the new behaviors until they became habits ingrained in their way of doing things. Thus, within the first six months the program could show considerable success to government officials. Monique's and her husband's visas were renewed, and the program went on. The story illustrates how to look for positive deviance in situations where the solution, and the process to find the solution, is unknown. Monique needed to find a very low cost and timely solution to move forward within an adverse environment where resources were quite limited. The search for positive deviance offered a low-cost solution to the adverse situation found in an unfamiliar environment.

Serving as an embedded ally. An example of working in a complex environment comes to us from Sheryl Dahl, who was searching for a solution to the problem of global over fishing. She started out as a researcher and consultant, but eventually founded an entrepreneurial activity called the Future of Fish initiative. In her new role, she describes herself as an embedded ally in the system. The supply chain for getting the commercial fishing catch to market is a system that involves all of the normal complexity of a system with many actors — including the fishermen, wholesalers, restaurants, and consumers. Initially, Sheryl sent out anthropologists to look at the existing supply chain, and to map out how things were working within the system. What they found were many logical decisions that were being made based on the unique self-interest of the participants; what some would describe as simply the normal way of doing things.

The problem was that on the demand-side, restaurants and the patrons of the restaurants were always asking for the same five fish species, which included the names of well-known fish that you might expect to find in a restaurant. Of course, that's not how the environment works, as far as the fisherman's catch goes. Many other kinds of fish are available at different times of the year, from different locations in the fish supply chain. Thus, there was often a mismatch between the fish that were available and the fish that were being asked for in the restaurants. Because of this mismatch, there was considerable incentive for mislabeling of fish in the system. About one-third of seafood is said to be mislabeled, and in sushi restaurants it's much higher.

One example that illustrates the problem is Maryland blue crab. At some times of the year, the crab sold in Maryland as Blue Crab was coming in from Indonesia, but was still being sold as Maryland Blue Crab. The Future of Fish initiative set up a chef training program that would guarantee the supply chain from the Maryland distributors that had authentic Blue Crab. They trained the chefs in how to recognize and prepare authentic Maryland crab, and how to get it at appropriate times during the year. By being an embedded ally within the system, the Future of Fish initiative could see the problems of supply and demand up close, and then act to help sort out the issues between suppliers and consumers. The program has been successful and is still going on. The benefit so far has been to change some of the incentives and resulting behaviors of actors in the system so that supply and demand can be more easily matched. This example offers an approach for the knowledge worker facing a difficult situation within a complex environment.

Co-creating a solution. Let me provide a story from my own experience, working in an (culturally) unknown environment. In the 1980s I found myself working in South Asia with the World Health Organization during the first UN Water Decade. One of the problems in the Republic of Maldives was the lack of latrines that women felt comfortable using. Instead of using an engineering design which was likely to fail, we involved sociologists and other social scientists in the effort to work with small groups of women. The women (working with the sociologists) described the kind of experience they liked to have by the seashore looking at the open sky early in the morning. So, the team designed a latrine with four compartments, each open to the sky, and with a central well in the middle where you could draw water for washing hands, and for other things that would be needed to maintain the cleanliness of the facilities.

The design was a success, and was replicated elsewhere in the country. It offers an example of a co-creation effort that may be required when the knowledge worker faces a culturally unfamiliar environment.

Programming the organization for effectiveness

Our earlier discussion contrasted aspects of manual work and knowledge work, two extremes on a wide spectrum. The manual workers that Taylor studied were unskilled laborers, not the skilled artisans of his day. When industry created a job for a manual worker, the factory owned the means of production (the equipment), determined the relevance of the worker's input to the finished product, and determined how the task would be accomplished (i.e., via Taylor's methods).

Today's knowledge workers are vastly different. It is the knowledge worker who owns the means of production (the knowledge), determines the relevance of his/her input to the finished product or service, and has significant control over how the task is defined and how the work accomplished. This knowledge goes home every night with the worker, and an asset is lost to the organization if the worker does not return in the morning.

The risks of the goal model. How can we program the work of the organization so that it is done in an efficient and effective manner, no matter the type of work or worker? The traditional approach to organizing the work is for management to set up a particular organizational form (organizational chart), program the units with a series of goals and objectives, then lead and direct the staff to fulfill them. The is the basic idea behind Management by Objectives (Drucker [1954/1982] 1993), and variations thereof, that utilizes the goal model for effectiveness. The problem with this approach is that the goal model will accept almost any goal that management wishes to throw at it, and not all goals have any relation to improvements in effectiveness. It is difficult to know whether the right goal has been specified, and even if the goal is achieved, it may not mean that the organization is effective.

Selecting a new executive team with a new set of goals can be a risky strategy with unpredictable results. In 1974, Peter Drucker wrote in response to a rash of reorganizations in large American organizations, "the main causes of instability are *changes in the objective task,* in the kind of business and institution to be organized. This is at the root of the crisis of organization practice" (Drucker 1974). As an extension to our Chapter 1 on efficiencyism, the more single-minded an organization becomes in focusing on a narrow financial objective (such as maximization of profit or shareholder value) at the expense of everything else, the more likely it is that dysfunction will emerge.

The situation can become a national crisis if an entire sector is doing the same thing. For example, the financial debacle of 2006-2008 and beyond in the USA was precipitated by investment banks that were focused on generating financial profits from complex investment vehicles in the housing market, without the vehicles being sufficiently supported by underlying assets on their books — thus increasing market risks and increasing environmental instability over time (eventually leading to a crisis). The rise of instability in organizational systems may explain why the risk of exit for public companies traded in the US now stands at 32 percent over 5 years, compared with the 5 percent risk that they would have faced 50 years ago (Reeves and Pueschel 2015). For individual public companies, these exits are mostly unintended and are likely associated with managerial failure.

How M+OE programs the organization for effectiveness. Instead of using the goal model, let's consider how the organization is programmed under Management by Positive Organizational Effectiveness (using the OFM). In this case, the selection of the organization's goal has already been made, because the goal of every organization (under the OFM) is the same, that is, to be effective within its environment. The pursuit of this single goal avoids the inherent conflict that results from the pursuit of multiple goals simultaneously within an organization, which is a common problem (Ethiraj and Levinthal 2009).

Under M+OE, the effectiveness of the organization as a whole is about the effectiveness of its *portfolio* of results chains (one for each offering). Instead of being programmed by top management, the results chains can be programmed by small teams of workers that know the outcomes that are expected. Here, management's role is to provide clear direction by defining success, resources, constraints, and the guiding principles to be followed. Otherwise, they can step back and let the teams do their work.

Despite the greater autonomy of the knowledge worker in the production process, the organization (and its management) is still relevant in programming knowledge work. The organization needs to provide the processes necessary to properly sequence the tasks and distribute them to the knowledge workers in a logical, timely, and efficient manner. It also manages, oversees and coordinates the team work needed to guarantee attributes of overall quality. Finally, and of critical importance (under M+OE), it is responsible for monitoring the external environment to gather feedback on how the outputs are being received (i.e., EEO behaviors). The entire system helps to program the organization and its workers for both efficiency and effectiveness.

If a team of knowledge workers knows what outcomes (EEOs) are desired or expected within a results chain, they can work backward to design an offering, then pilot the offering to test demand-side response. Under the M+OE, management delegates the responsibility for serving the customer directly to the product or service team or division, giving them the discretion and resources needed to program their work. This frees top management to serve as the coach, evaluator and banker — deciding which new initiatives, products and services will be funded, evaluating how well existing offerings are performing, and when mature offerings should be discontinued. The more that the organization is in tune with the needs of its demand-side environment over time, the more successful it can be in adapting its offerings for continued effectiveness when change occurs, and in programming the organization (no matter the type of work or worker).

One occasionally hears calls for large corporations to move toward longer-term measures of performance to better manage their operations, downplaying the need for quarterly financial reporting. These calls have generally fallen on deaf ears. M+OE has a better, more lasting solution. EEOs provide immediate short-term feedback on a daily, even hourly, basis for those managers willing to focus on indicators of effectiveness, and to learn from the evolving behavior of demand-side actors. Close attention to what consumers are doing (and saying) is a kind of truth that management is well advised to cherish. Entering the Age of Organizational Effectiveness, in fact, demands it.

CHAPTER 16

BECOME TRULY GREAT
(PHASE 3 OF M+OE)

This book has invited you to embark on a journey from the current age of efficiencyism to the Age of Organizational Effectiveness. In the new age, organizations serve their environment and are rewarded in return. We have stated that the goal of every organization (whether business, government, or nonprofit) is to be effective within its environment, while strengthening the whole (the common good). Previous chapters have outlined a three-phase path to greatness: Be Virtuous, Discover Effectiveness, Become Truly Great.

In Phase 1, Be Virtuous, your organization examines its values in order to embed and retain the positive values necessary to achieve and sustain true greatness.

In Phase 2, Discover Effectiveness, your organization defines and tests the results chains associated with each of its existing and proposed offerings to calibrate and gauge their effectiveness (while maintaining the values embedded and retained in Phase 1). By the end of Phase 2, you will have come far, and your environment is already rewarding you.

In Phase 3, Become Truly Great, an organization serves its environment so well that it becomes integral to it, securely occupying one or more niche(s), and improving the health of the environment as a whole.

Phase 3 organizations need to be consistently effective for at least 5 years to attain true greatness, working to improve their processes (and retaining the values) that have been developed on the journey thus far. Truly great organizations are integral (if not indispensable) to their environment. They consistently build up (rather than tear down) the surrounding ecosystem and help make their niche more resilient. Being truly great is not about 'winning,' which implies that someone else is 'losing.' Rather, it is about being recognized by your environment as being great among, and of service to, your fellow actors in the environment. Greatness can take different forms, depending upon the size and focus of an organization's niche – resulting in organizations that are locally great, regionally great, nationally great, or internationally great.

In this, the last chapter of the book, let me note that other authors have written about the topic of organizational 'greatness' in one form or another. For instance, Jim Collins has been one of the most popular authors of the last few decades. He (along with his coauthors) has written books such as *Built to Last* (Collins and Porras 1994), *Good to Great* (J. Collins 2001), *How the Mighty Fall* (J. Collins 2009), and *Great by Choice* (Collins and Hansen 2011). The approach used (characterized by *Good to Great*) was to look at companies listed on the US stock market, tracking their performance over a period of years to see which ones had done the best (mostly in terms of market performance among their peers). This provided a list of companies that were rated as doing very well. Then, other companies were highlighted that didn't do as well, but were similar to those on the first list, to use as a control group, contrasting the superior performance (the 'great' ones), with ones that were not so great. It's an approach that elevates stock market performance to the main determinant of greatness. The approach has been criticized by scholars who point out that in *Good to Great*, Collins used data mining techniques to find companies that passed certain performance filters, but failed to prove that the five principles of greatness derived from that cohort held up in other circumstances (Niendorf and Beck 2008). Collins's approach is not the approach that we have taken in this book, by any means, but I wanted to mention Jim Collins to highlight one view of greatness that readers may be familiar with.

Another author writing in this area is Tom Peters, who has written popular books over the last few decades on organizational excellence. His series includes, *In Search of Excellence* (Peters and Waterman 1982), *A Passion for Excellence* (Peters and Austin 1985), *Thriving on Chaos* (T. Peters 1987), *The Pursuit of Wow* (T. J. Peters 1994), and *The Little Big Things* (2010) (T. J. Peters 2010). The approach that Tom Peters and his co-authors used in their series was primarily anecdotal, involving storytelling. His recommendations, he says himself, often offered "blindingly obvious" prescriptions such as staying close to the customer, doing little things well, and being passionate about serving customers. He uses interesting examples from wide variety of organizations to illustrate points in the books. He also advocates "Management by Wandering Around" (MBWA) to stay close to the customer, and to stay close to employees by interacting informally on a regular basis. The approach of presenting the reader with a myriad of examples is what I would call "management philosophy by induction." As in inductive reasoning, his arguments provide premises which give grounds for conclusions, but do not necessitate them. Less clear, however, is how anecdotal story-telling is converted into useful organizational theory that can be applied in a predictive manner.

A 2013 article in the *Harvard Business Review* listed two foundational principles for making a company truly great: (1) better before cheaper, and (2) revenue before cost (Raynor and Ahmed 2013), based on a statistical review of several thousand companies. The authors suggest in the first instance that it is better for a company to differentiate its offerings to provide unique value, rather than to compete on price. In the second rule, which is complementary to the first, the suggestion is that top line revenue growth (by improving traction in the marketplace) should be the main priority instead of trying to cut costs by doing "more with less." *Become Truly Great* (the book) does not conflict with either of these principles, but offers an alternative approach to attain greatness.

I have tried to come to the topics in this book in a way that serves both theory and practice. Judgments regarding how successful my efforts have been in serving those ends must be left to others. The intention has been to provide readers with an understanding of true greatness (including organizational effectiveness) in a practical sense, so that managers can begin to apply useful principles in their thinking on Monday morning. Throughout the book, I have titled this new approach, Management by Positive Organizational Effectiveness (M+OE).

Compared to current management practices, M+OE differs in a few key areas:

1. M+OE discards the goal model that has been used prominently to gauge organizational performance and effectiveness, because it does not provide a way to discriminate between useful and non-useful

goals. Within M+OE, by contrast, the goal of every organization is fixed, that is, to be effective within its environment. Organizations that consider their goals to be the maximization of profit, shareholder value, or other such goals driven primarily by financial/economic gain are not using M+OE. They are still living in an age of efficiencyism, where dysfunction is an emergent phenomenon (due to potential instability within an organization's complex adaptive system).

2. M+OE uses the outcome-focused model (OFM, Chapter 7) to gage effectiveness within individual results chains, and overall effectiveness from the organization's portfolio of results chains. Expected external outcomes (EEOs) serve as objective referents for the direct observation of effectiveness in the field. EEOs are demand-side behaviors of customers and other actors that validate effectiveness in each results chain, thus verifying that the supply-side of the organization is offering what the demand side willingly takes up, adopts, and uses.

3. M+OE counsels the incorporation of positive values within the organization from the start, to attract & amplify success, instill virtuousness, and be protective on the journey toward greatness.

4. M+OE offers a way to make both manual workers and knowledge workers productive. While Taylor's "scientific management" enabled manual worker productivity by increasing task efficiency through time and motion studies, the OFM enables the production of internal outputs and their conversion into expected external outcomes through the management of benefit exchanges at the supply/demand interface. M+OE programs the

organization for knowledge worker productivity because tasks can be specified once an offering's results chain and expected external outcome (EEO) have been determined.

5. M+OE encourages an organization, once it discovers effectiveness, to occupy one or more niches within its environment, and to serve the niche(s) so well that the competition is irrelevant. This is akin to a 'Blue Ocean' strategy rather than a 'Red Ocean' strategy (Kim and Mauborgne 2005), for readers familiar with the comparison.

6. M+OE encourages an organization to co-create value over time with stakeholders in its niche(s) in order to continuously adapt to environmental change and to serve the needs of the environment more fully (by offering the "requisite variety" of approaches needed for successful adaptation within a changing environment). In this way, a pipeline of new offerings can emerge to replace mature products and services that become outdated, or to expand offerings in promising new areas. Observations of demand-side behavior are instructive as feedback to hone the preferred attributes of an organization's offerings over time.

7. Within M+OE, effectiveness is an instantaneous measure that can be observed in the field every day (or measured periodically, as appropriate). True greatness, on the other hand, is the longer-term and cumulative *impact* of effectiveness that is associated with an organization's reputation and impact over time. An organization can expect to spend at least five years applying the principles of effectiveness (while maintaining positive values) to become firmly established as a truly great organization in its chosen niche(s).

Since EEOs observed at the supply/demand interface are an instantaneous marker for effectiveness, they are subject to significant reduction during demand-shocks (e.g., during national or global economic crisis). An organization that is highly *efficient* in turning inputs to products and/services it sells may be deemed *ineffective* if a demand-shock puts the disposable income of society at risk, thus leading to lower sales. This is a valid and logical result from the OFM, and would serve as a wakeup call to management to find innovative ways to address the problem.

Utilizing M+OE within your organization means that product and service teams are empowered to consider a key question every day, "How can we serve our environment well today?" Businesses, government agencies and nonprofits have the same challenge. It's a probing question, and the answer may change over time. It's a question that will be difficult to answer quickly in a bureaucratic, top down, command-and-control management system. It is best handled by flexible, team-based management focused on the success of individual offerings to the environment by capable teams of knowledge workers. Of course, we are not suspending the principles of accounting, economics, or finance, in making such decisions, but these are not necessarily constraints. Like Tom Peters' approach, it focuses on staying close to the customer, wandering around (e.g., watching for expected demand-side behaviors), and being passionate about serving. M+OE provides a clear view of what demand-side success looks like (through EEOs). To the extent that the approach generates true greatness, it is likely to deliver superior financial and economic performance as well.

Does being truly great and occupying a niche mean that you don't have competitors? Perhaps not, but it does mean that you are paying attention to the big things and the little things that create effectiveness at the supply-demand interface, and that you are always testing new things to serve your environment better. So, why isn't the goal of every organization to be great rather than to be effective? Well, because an organization needs to focus on something that can be observed every day, to provide feedback and correction. Greatness (and superior reward) is something that is a natural outgrowth of being effective over time, together with serving your environment using positive values.

Truly great organizations know their environment well and serve it effectively with their offerings. They closely monitor demand-side behaviors to determine if the environment is behaving as expected, to be alert for emerging new behaviors that need to be studied further. Once an organization has developed and tested a portfolio of results chains (with more in the pipeline), it has the keys within hand to survive and thrive. Continuous adaptation to the environment is critical for survival, since the danger over the mid- to long-term is that the environment will change in ways that make the organization's offerings irrelevant. Major catastrophic events such as 9/11 (or the 2008 recession in the US) can compress this timeframe, of course, and make the need for an appropriate response immediate.

We began our journey by noting that efficiencyism is holding organizations back from achieving their true potential. Dysfunction is an emergent phenomenon under efficiencyism because the goal model allows the use of arbitrary goals that can elevate efficiency to a prime directive without an appreciation of its assumptions and consequences. The single-minded pursuit of profit, shareholder value, or any other objective (other than effectively serving your external environment, and improving the whole) can create instability within an organization's complex adaptive system for a variety of reasons. It is likely to be more rewarding and stabilizing over the mid- to long-term to entertain the creation of social capital, psychological capital, spiritual capital, and environmental capital among stakeholders – thus encouraging the emergence of attractor narratives (e.g., in social media and elsewhere) based on real benefit exchanges. Nonprofits have shown the way forward in these areas.

Evolutionary processes operate on the population of organizations, while adaptive pressures act on individual organizations, to enforce "survival of the effective" over time. We have seen that ineffective organizations are marginalized or eliminated by their environment in the absence of a sufficient exchange of benefits across the supply/demand interface. Organizations that intentionally harbor negative values are continually at risk, and can become unstable and short lived once the environment recognizes and rejects their corrosive attributes, then actively engages in efforts to expose and eliminate the offenders among them.

The Age of Organizational Effectiveness will arrive when C-suite teams and other executives and managers "think different" using the principles outlined in this book, and efficiencyism gives way to positive organizational effectiveness – one organization at a time. In the new age, small and large organizations alike (whether business, government, or nonprofit) will serve their environment and be rewarded in return, thus managing capitalism for the common good. Truly great organizations add more to the world than they extract (Schwartz 2013). The world needs organizations that are virtuous, effective, and truly great. It will not be possible to solve the myriad problems that society now faces without them. This is the challenge of true greatness under M+OE.

My passion is for 10,000 organizations to begin the journey to "Become Truly Great" by the year 2025. Are you ready to join a movement? If so, visit www.BecomeTrulyGreat.com to get started.

EPILOGUE

This book was in the gestation phase for a long time. Many of the ideas on a new way to think about management (and effectiveness, in particular) have come from my experience in international development since the early 1980's. During the early part of the UN's International Drinking Water Supply and Sanitation Decade (IDWSSD), 1981-1990, I was living in New Delhi, India, with my family where I was working in the regional office of the World Health Organization on a project funded by UNDP. As the project manager, my job was to advise participating governments in South Asia on how to create successful projects for the delivery of water supply and sanitation services. I traveled around the region (Indonesia, Sri Lanka, India, Bangladesh, Maldives, Nepal, Thailand) and observed projects at close range. The underlying problem was that the goal for the UN Water Decade focused on coverage targets (the percentage of the population that had access to clean water and adequate sanitation), so governments had interpreted their job as one of simply building facilities to deliver water and sanitation services to as many people as possible. The basic idea was simple: "We" will build it, and "they" will use it.

The IDWSSD started off as a game of numbers, with coverage targets driving the discussion, and participating countries made a good deal of new funding available to address the needs. A flurry of activity was begun in country after country by government agencies, stringing pipes in rural areas, building household latrines, and increasing the number of wells. Unfortunately, many those early facilities either quickly broke down for lack of maintenance, or were not used for their intended purposes (e.g., latrines storing hay, drainage ditches filled with trash). Government agencies thought that they knew what the people wanted. They had been doing the job for years. But there was a gap between the planners and the people that could benefit from their efforts. The supply side didn't understand the demand side. Focusing on deliverables (outputs) alone resulted in a lot of broken down and abandoned facilities. Clearly, project success was not about supplying pipes, pumps, and latrines, it was about much more.

For success in rural water supply and sanitation, it was clear that we had to get the users involved in designing the facilities, what has come to be called participatory design. WHO came to believe that success was a three-phase process involving coverage, functioning, and utilization. Coverage was only the first phase, but it involved participatory design, so that the gap between people and planners was reduced. The criteria for success included not only coverage of the population by providing access to facilities, but the continued functioning and utilization of the facilities, as well.

As the Decade moved on, I came to believe that I understood what effectiveness was, at least in projects. Projects that were focused only on supplying facilities (i.e., delivering outputs on the supply side) were problematic. Among these, I saw lots of projects that were poorly conceived and were failing in the field. Projects focused on outputs alone didn't worry about demand-side response. For success, project objectives needed to focus on demand-side outcomes (uptake, adoption and use of the outputs). Outputs did not lead to expected outcomes unless the expected outcomes themselves became the objective. I decided that it was necessary to clearly distinguish the supply side from the demand side, then set the objective on the achievement of demand-side behaviors that would validate the results chain hypothesis. Later this led me to a principle that I call Chandler's Razor: "outputs without their associated and expected outcomes are largely waste, because one or more results chains have failed."

Since those early days in South Asia with WHO, I have had the chance to see hundreds of projects prepared by the largest development agencies in the world in all sectors (e.g., education, health, power, transport, etc.). I was offered the opportunity to introduce the logical framework to the World Bank in 1997, at a time when it was being adopted in all new operations, and I subsequently helped with the conceptual design of over 800 projects being funded by the World Bank Group (including IBRD, IDA, MIGA, and IFC).

Projects may change, but common problems remain. In the end, an effective project is one that achieves expected external outcomes in the demand-side environment. It's what the economic and financial analyses assumed to be true from the start. Unfortunately, not all development agencies understand outcomes in the same way (i.e., demand-side response). A large percentage of development projects still have objectives that focus on outputs under the control of the project, rather than on external outcomes. Even some of the Millennium Development Goals for 2015 focused on outputs on the supply side (e.g., access to services) rather than on demand-side outcomes (e.g., uptake, adoption, and use).

In this book, I have expanded my analysis of the problem of organizational effectiveness beyond temporary organizations (as I have experienced them in institutions of international development), to permanent organizations in the private and nonprofit sectors, and in government. When I began expanded research on organizational effectiveness (about 2008), I was surprised to discover that scholars had abandoned the OE construct after the mid-1980s due to a high level of disagreement surrounding its definition. In the disagreement, however, I saw some hope that my experience with temporary organizations could provide a new view of effectiveness useful to both practitioners and scholars.

The potential role of a new concept of organizational effectiveness has long been recognized by scholars – a role in which OE would function as a capstone concept in organizational theory and draw together several disparate areas into a unified whole. Whether my views on OE can serve this role, I will leave to others to judge. I hope you find M+OE to be a useful approach, with direct applicability to your organization.

Charles G. Chandler, Ph.D.

REFERENCES

Aldrich, H. 1979. *Organizations and Environments*. Englewood Cliffs, NJ: Prentice-Hall.

Amaeshi, Kenneth, Paul Nnodim, and Onyeka Osuji. 2013. *Corporate social responsibility, entrepreneurship, and innovation.* New York, NY: Routledge.

AMJ editors. 2014. "Organizations with Purpose." *Academy of Management Journal* 57 (5): 1227-1234.

Anderson, J. C., M. Rungtusanatham, and R. Schroeder. 1994. "A theory of quality management underlying the Deming management method." *Academy of Management Review* 19: 472-509.

Asian Development Bank. 2006. "An introduction to results management: Principles, implications, and applications." Manila, Philippines.

Azarian, B. 2016. "Why digital computers can't have consciousness." *Huffington Post*, June 2.

Barnard, Chester I. 1938. *The Functions of the Executive.* 1968 edition. Cambridge, MA: Harvard University Press.

Bauman, Z., and T. May. 2001. *Thinking sociologically.* Oxford, England: Blackwell Publishers.

Benioff, Marc. 2015. "A Call for Stakeholder Activists." *Huffington Post,* February 2, online ed.

Best, M., and D. Neuhauser. 2005. "W. Edwards Deming: Father of quality management, patient and composer." *Qual Saf Health Care* 14: 310-312.

Bluedorn, A. C. 1980. "Cutting the Gordian knot: A critique of the effectiveness tradition in organization research." *Sociology and Social Research* 64: 477-496.

Brandenburger, A. M., and H. W. Stuart. 1996. "Value-based Business Strategy." *Journal of Economics and Management Strategy* 5 (1): 5-24.

Burke, James. 1985. *The Day the Universe Changed.* Boston, MA: Little, Brown & Company.

Bush Administration. 2008. *Expectmore.gov.*

Cameron, Kim S. (Ed.). 2010. *Organizational Effectiveness.* Northampton, MA: Edwin Elgar.

Cameron, Kim S. 1986. "Effectiveness as paradox: Consensus and conflict in conceptions of organizational effectiveness." *Management Science* 32: 539-553.

Cameron, Kim S. 1978. "Measuring organizational effectiveness in institutions of higher education." *Administrative Science Quarterly* 23: 604-632.

Cameron, Kim S. 2005. "Organizational effectiveness." In *Great minds in management,* edited by K. G. Smith and M. A Hitt, 304-330. New York, NY: Oxford University Press.

Cameron, Kim S. 1981. *The enigma of organizational effectiveness.* Reprint series, Boulder, CO: National Center for Higher Education Management Systems.

Cameron, Kim S., and David A. Whetten (Eds.). 1983. *Organizational effectiveness: A comparison of multiple models.* Orlando, FL: Academic Press, Inc.

Cameron, Kim S., and David A. Whetten. 1996. *Organizational effectiveness and quality: The second generation.* Vol. XI, in *Higher education: Handbook of theory and research,* 265-306. New York, NY: Agathon.

Cameron, Kim S., J. E. Dutton, and R. E. Quinn. 2003. "Chapter 1: An Introduction to Positive Organizational Scholarship." In *Positive Organizational Scholarship.* San Francisco, CA: Berrett-Koehler.

Caraher, Lee. 2015. *Millennials & Management: The Essential Guide to Making It Work at Work.* Brookline, MA: Bibliomotion.

Center for Ethical Business Cultures. 2010. " Corporate Social Responsibility: The Shape of a History, 1945-2004." Working Paper #1, Minneapolis, MN.

Chandler, Alfred D. (Jr.). 1977. *The Visible Hand: The Managerial Revolution in American Business.* Cambridge, MA: Belknap Press.

Chandler, Charles G. 2015. "Organizational Effectiveness: Replacing a Vague Construct with a Defined Concept." *Academy of Management Proceedings* 2015: 11023.

Chouinard, Yvon, and Naomi Klein. 2005/2016. *Let my people go surfing: The education of a reluctant businessman.* New York, NY: Penguin Books.

Coase, Ronald. 1937. "The Nature of the Firm." *Economica* 4 (16): 386-405.

Coleman, J. S. 1991. "Constructed organization: First principles." *J. Law Econom.* 7: 7-23.

—. 1990. *Foundations of social theory.* Cambridge, MA: Belknap Press of Harvard University Press.

Collins, J., and M. T. Hansen. 2011. *Great by Choice: Uncertainty, Chaos, and Luck — Why Some Thrive Despite Them All*. New York, NY: HarperCollins.

Collins, James. 2001. *Good to Great: Why Some Companies Make the Leap & Others Don't*. New York, NY: HarperCollins.

—. 2009. *How the Mighty Fall: And Why Some Companies Never Give In*. New York, NY: HarperCollins.

Collins, James, and Jerry I. Porras. 1994. *Built to Last: Successful Habits of Visionary Companies*. New York, NY: HarperCollins.

Connolly, T. A., E. J. Conlon, and S. J. Deutsch. 1980. "Organizational effectiveness: A multiple constituency approach." *Academy of Management Review* 5: 211-218.

Copernicus, Nicholas. [1543] 1995. *On the revolutions of heavenly spheres*. 1995 edition. Amherst, NY: Prometheus Books.

Czarniawska, B. 1997. *Narrating the organization: Dramas of institutional identity*. Chicago, IL: University of Chicago Press.

Dan, A. 2012. "Kodak Failed by Asking the Wrong Marketing Question." *Forbes*, January 23, online ed.

Dao, J. 2001. "Ads now seek recruits for 'An Army of One.'" *New York Times*, January 10.

Dean, A., and M. Kretschmer. 2007. "Can Ideas be Capital? Factors of Production in the Postindustrial Economy: A Review and Critique." *Academy of Management Review* 32 (2): 573-594.

Dean, J. W., and D. E. Bowen. 1994. "Management theory and total quality: Improving research and practice through theory development." *Academy of Management Review* 19: 392-418.

Deci, E. L., and R. M. Ryan. 1985. *Intrinsic motivation and self-determination in human behavior*. New York, NY: Plenum.

Deming, W. Edwards. 1982. *Out of the Crisis*. Cambridge, MA: MIT Press.

Dennett, D. C. 1987. *The Intentional Stance*. Cambridge, MA: MIT Press.

Denning, S., J. Goldstein, and M. Pacanowsky. 2015. "Scrum Alliance: The Learning Consortium for the Creative Economy, 2015 Report." Presented at the Drucker Forum, Vienna, Austria.

Denning, Steven. 2012. "Don't miss the paradigm shift in management...it's happening." *Forbes*, October 31, online ed.

—. 2011a. "The Five Big Surprises of Radical Management." *Forbes*, July 8, online ed.

—. 2016a. "What's wrong with big business?" *Forbes*, April 11, online ed.

—. 2014. "Why IBM is in Decline." *Forbes*, May 30, online ed.

—. 2011b. "Why Shared Value Can't Fix Capitalism." *Forbes*, December 20, online ed.

—. 2016b. "Why We Live in a Second Robber Baron Era." *Forbes*, April 30, online ed.

Drucker, Peter F. 1974. "New Templates for Today's Organizations." *Harvard Business Review*, January, online ed.

—. 1999a. *Management Challenges for the 21st Century*. New York, NY: HarperCollins.

—. 1973. *Management: Tasks, Responsibilities, Practices*. New York, NY: Harper & Row.

Drucker, Peter F. 1999b. "The deadly sins in public administration." In *Public sector performance: Management, motivation and measurement*, edited by R. Kearney and E. Berman. Boulder, CO: Westview Press.

—. 1966. *The Effective Executive*. New York, NY: HarperCollins.

—. [1954/1982] 1993. *The Practice of Management*. 1993 Harper Business edition. New York, NY: HarperCollins.

Ethiraj, S. K., and D. Levinthal. 2009. "Hoping for A to Z while rewarding only A: Complex organizations and multiple goals." *Organization Science* 20 (1): 4-21.

Friedman, Milton. 1970. "The Social Responsibility of Business is to Increase Its Profits." *New York Times Magazine*, September 13.

Garvin, D. A. 1988. *Managing quality: The strategic and competitive edge*. New York, NY: The Free Press.

Gavetti, G., D. Levinthal, and W. Ocasio. 2007. "Neo-Carnegie: The Carnegie School's past, present, and reconstructing for the future." *Organization Science* 18: 523-536.

Gittell, J., K. Cameron, and S. Lim. 2005. "Relationships, Layoffs and Organizational Resilience: Airline Industry Responses to September 11." *The Journal of Applied Behavioral Science* 42: 300-328.

Glinton, S. 2015. "How a little lab in West Virginia Caught Volkswagen's Big Cheat." *NPR*, September 24, online ed.

Glynn, Mary Ann. 2016. "Making Organizations Meaningful - Academy of Management Annual Meeting 2016." *AOM.org*.

Glynn, Matt. 2014. "Ex-Southwest Airlines CEO Offers Lessons in Leadership from Post 9/11 Crisis." *Buffalo News*, May 19, online ed.

Goodman, P. S., R. S. Atkin, and F. D. Schoorman. 1983. "On the demise of organizational effectiveness studies." In *Organizational effectiveness: A comparison of multiple models*, edited by K. S. Cameron and D. A. Whetten. New York, NY: Academic Press.

Grant, E. X. 2006. "TWA — The Death of a Legend." *St. Louis Magazine*, July 28, online ed.

Hakimi, S. 2015. "Why Purpose-Driven Companies Are Often More Successful." *Fast Company*, July 21, online ed.

Hammer, Michael, and James Champy. 1993. *Reengineering the Corporation: A Manifesto for Business Revolution*. New York, NY: HarperCollins.

Hannan, M. T., and J. Freeman. 1989. *Organizational Ecology*. Cambridge, MA: Harvard University Press.

Hannan, M. T., and J. Freeman. 1977. "The population ecology of organizations." *American Journal of Sociology* 82: 929-964.

Hess, E. D., and Kim S. Cameron (Eds.). 2006. *Leading with Values: Positivity, Virtue, and High Performance*. Cambridge, England: Cambridge University Press.

Hirsch, P. M., and D. Z. Levin. 1999. "Umbrella advocates versus validity police: A life-cycle model." *Organization Science* 10: 199-213.

Honeyman, R. 2014. "Has the B Corp Movement Made a Difference?" *Stanford Social Innovation Review*, October 13, online ed.

Hormby, T. 2013. "Think Different: The Ad Campaign that Restored Apple's Reputation." *Lowendmac.com*. August 10.

Hrebiniak, L. G. 1978. *Complex Organizations*. St. Paul, MN: West Publishing Company.

Kahn, R. L. 1977. "Organizational effectiveness: An overview." In *New perspectives on organizational effectiveness*, edited by P. S. Goodman et al. San Francisco: Jossey-Bass.

Kantor, J., and S. Streitfeld. 2015. "Inside Amazon: Wrestling Ideas in a Bruising Workplace." *New York Times*, August 15, online ed.

Kay, J. 2015. "Shareholders think they own the company — they are wrong." *Financial Times*, November 10, online ed.

Kellogg Foundation. 2004. *Logic model development guide.* Battle Creek, MI: W. K. Kellogg Foundation.

Kim, W. Chan, and Renee Mauborgne. 2005. *Blue Ocean Strategy: How to Create Uncontested Market Space and Make Competition Irrelevant.* Cambridge, MA: Harvard Business School Publishing.

Kimes, M. 2013. "At Sears, Eddie Lampert's Warring Divisions Model Adds to the Troubles." *Bloomberg*, July 11, online ed.

King, Brayden D., Teppo Felin, and David A. Whetten. 2010. "Finding the organization in organizational theory: A meta-theory of the organization as social actor." *Organization Science* 21: 290-305.

Komori, S. 2015. *Innovating Out of Crisis: How Fujifilm survived (and thrived) as its core business was vanishing.* Berkeley, CA: Stone Bridge Press.

Kuhn, Thomas. 1962. *The Structure of Scientific Revolutions.* Chicago, IL: University ofChicago Press.

Lane, N. 2015. *The Vital Question: Energy, Evolution, and the Origin of Complex Life.* New York, NY: W. W. Norton & Co.

Lazonick, W. 2014. "Profits Without Prosperity." *Harvard Business Review,* September 2014, online ed.

Lewin, K. 1951. "Problems of research in social psychology." In *Field Theory in Social Science: Selected Theoretical Papers,* edited by D. Cartwright, 155-169. New York, NY: Harper & Row.

Lichtenstein, Benyamin B. 2016. "Complexity Science at a Crossroads: Exploring the Science of Emergence." *Academy of Management Proceedings* 2016: 12259.

Loehr, A. 2015. "The Future of Work: Creating Purpose-Driven Organizations." *The Huffington Post,* Februray 26, online ed.

Morgan, G. 1980. "Paradigms, metaphors, and puzzle-solving in organizational theory." *Administrative Science Quarterly* 25: 605-622.

Mourkogiannis, N. 2006. *Purpose: The Starting Point of Great Companies.* New York, NY: Palgrave MacMillan.

Niendorf, B., and K. Beck. 2008. "Good to Great, or just Good?" *Academy of Management Perspectives* 22 (4): 13-20.

NORAD. 1999. *The logical framework approach: Handbook for objectives-oriented planning.* 4th edition. Peterson AFB, CO: NORAD.

Oppel, R. A., and A. R. Sorkin. 2001. "Enron's collapse: The Overview; Enron Corp. files largest US claim for bankruptcy." *New York Times,* December 3.

Peters, Thomas J. 2010. *The Little Big Things: 163 Ways to Pursue Excellence.* New York, NY: HarperCollins.

—. 1994. *The Pursuit of Wow! Every Person's Guide to Topsy-Turvy Times.* New York, NY: Random House.

Peters, Thomas. 1987. *Thriving on Chaos: Handbook for a Management Revolution.* New York, NY: Alfred A. Knopf, Inc.

Peters, Thomas, and Nancy Austin. 1985. *A Passion for Excellence: The Leadership Difference.* New York, NY: Random House.

Peters, Thomas, and R. H. Waterman. 1982. *In Search of Excellence: Lessons from America's Best Run Companies.* New York, NY: HarperCollins.

Pfeffer, J., and G. R. Salancik. 1978. *The external control of organizations.* New York, NY: Harper & Row.

Porter, Michael, and Marc Kramer. 2011. "Creating Shared Value." *Harvard Business Review,* January-February 2011: 63-77.

Porter, Michael, Greg Hills, Marc Pfitzer, Sonja Patscheke, and Elizabeth Hawkins. n.d. *Measuring Shared Value.* Boston, MA: FSG, Inc.

Price, J. L. 1968. *Organizational effectiveness: An inventory of propositions.* Homewood, IL: Richard D. Irwin, Inc.

Price, J. L. 1972. "The study of organizational effectiveness." *Sociological Quarterly* 13: 3-15.

Quinn, R. E., and J. Rohrbaugh. 1981. "A competing values approach to organizational effectiveness." *Public Productivity Review* 5: 122-140.

Radio Lab Podcast. 2016. "Cellmates." April 6.

Raynor, Michael E., and Mumtaz Ahmed. 2013. "Three rules for making a company truly great." *Harvard Business Review,* April 2013, online ed.

Reed, E. 2016. "How Economic Austerity Led Flint, Michigan Astray." *Mainstreet.com,* January 22, online ed.

Reeves, M., and L. Pueschel. 2015. "Die another day: What leaders can do about the shrinking life expectancy of corporations." *BCG Perspectives,* July 2, online ed.

Rogers, Patricia J. 2008. "Using Programme Theory to Evaluate Complicated and Complex Aspects of Interventions." *Evaluation* 14 (1): 29-48.

Rushe, D., and S. Thielman. 2015. "Google to restructure into new holding company called Alphabet." *The Guardian,* August 11, online ed.

Sainato, M. 2015. "Stephen Hawking, Elon Musk, and Bill Gates warn about artificial intelligence." *The Observer,* August 19, online ed.

Schaefer, S., and C. Wickert. 2015. "The Efficiency Paradox in Organization and Management Theory." *Academy of Management Proceedings* 2015: 10958.

Scharmer, Otto. 2015. "MITx u.Lab: Education as activating social fields." *Huffington Post,* December 22, online ed.

Schwartz, Tony. 2013. "Truly great companies add more than they extract." *New York Times,* June 7, online ed.

Scott, W. R. 1992. *Organizations: Rational, natural, and open systems.* 3rd edition. Englewood Cliffs, NJ: Prentice Hall.

Seashore, S. E., and E. Yuchtman. 1967. "Factorial analysis of organizational performance." *Administrative Science Quarterly* 12: 377-395.

Selznick, P. 1957. *Leadership in administration.* New York, NY: Harper and Row.

—. 1949. *TVA and the grass roots: A study in the sociology of formal organization.* New York, NY: Harper and Row.

Shenhav, Y., W. Shrum, and S. Alon. 1994. "'Goodness' concepts in the study of organizations: A longitudinal survey of four leading journals." *Organizational Studies* 15: 753-776.

Sherman, E. 2015. "Sears' CEO Erick Lampert should stop reading Ayn Rand." *Inc. Magazine*, April 20, online ed.

Sherman, G. 2016. "The Revenge of Roger's Angels." *New York Magazine*, September 2.

Skoll World Forum. 2013. "Game Changers: The World's Top Purpose-Driven Organizations." *Forbes*, November 4, online ed.

Smith, Adam. [1776] 2005. *An inquiry into the nature and causes of the wealth of nations.* 2005 edition, An Electronics Classics Series Publication. State College, PA: Pennsylvania State University.

Solari, Luca. 2016. *Freedom Management: How leaders can stay afloat in a sea of social connections.* Farnham (UK): Routledge.

Sozzi, B. 2016. "Qualcomm CEO — Here's what the next 30 years will look like for us." *The Street*, May 23, online ed.

Steers, R. M. 1975. "Problems in the measurement of organizational effectiveness." *Administrative Science Quarterly* 20: 546-558.

Stinchcombe, A. L. 1965. "Social structure and organizations." In *Handbook of organizations*, edited by J. G. March, 142-193. Chicago, IL: Rand McNally & Company.

Stout, Lynn A. 2002. "Bad and Not-so-Bad Arguments for Shareholder Primacy." *Southern California Law Review* 75: 1189-1209.

Taylor, Frederick Winslow. [1911] 1998. *The Principles of Scientific Management.* 1998 edition. Mineola, NY: Dover Publications.

Teather, D. 2005. "US Executive Pay Goes off the Scale." *The Guardian*, August 3, online ed.

The Economist staff. 2016a. "Shareholder value, analyze this: The enduring power of the biggest idea in business." *The Economist*, April 2.

—. 2012. "The Last Kodak Moment." *The Economist*, January 14, online ed.

—. 2008. "The Madoff Affair: Con of the Century." *The Economist*, December 18, online ed.

—. 2016b. "The Superstar Company, A Giant Problem." *The Economist*, September 17.

Thornton, M. 2009. "Cantillon and the Invisible Hand." *The Quarterly Journal of Australian Economics* 12 (2): 27-46.

ValueWalk staff. 2015. "The Case for and Against Activist Hedge Funds." *ValueWalk.com*. October 20.

Warren, Rick. 1995. *The Purpose-Driven Church*. Grand Rapids, MI: Zondervan.

Watt, J. H., and S. Van Den Berg. 1995. *Research methods for communication science*. Boston, MA: Allyn & Bacon.

Whetten, D. A. 2004. "In search of the 'O' in OMT." *Distinguished Scholar Address, Organization and Management Theory Division*. New Orleans, LA: Academy of Management annual meeting.

Wholey, J. S., H. P. Hatry, and K. E. Newcomer (Eds.). 2010. *Handbook of practical program evaluation*. San Francisco, CA: John Wiley & Sons.

Whoriskey, P. 2011. "Cozy relationships and 'peer benchmarking' send CEO pay soaring." *Washington Post*, October 3.

Zaheer, S., S. Albert, and A. Zaheer. 1999. "Time scales and organizational theory." *Academy of Management Review* 24: 725-741.

Zammuto, R. F. 1984. "A comparison of multiple constituency models of organizational effectiveness." *Academy of Management Review* 9: 606-616.

—. 1982. *Assessing organizational effectiveness: Systems change, adaptation, and strategy.* Albany, NY: SUNY Press.

ACKNOWLEDGEMENTS

I am an unlikely messenger for this book. All my university degrees list the department of engineering as my home. I began studying the formal management literature rather late in my career. As such, I don't view myself as an expert (or scholar) in the field of management, but rather a practitioner trying to explain (and extend) the body of knowledge for other practitioners.

My early views on management, along with those of many others, were influenced by the writings of Peter Drucker. I remember searching bookstores in New Delhi and Kathmandu to find Indian editions of his books when I lived in South Asia in the 1980s. In recent years, I have benefitted by getting to know the writings of scholars and practitioners that are members of the Academy of Management.

The impetus for my study of organizational effectiveness came from the writings of Kim Cameron and David Whetten, who have served as scholars, commentators, and observers of organizational effectiveness (OE) theory over the years. Their observations regarding the nature of OE as an enigma and wicked problem served to stir my interest, and set me on an investigative journey.

I did not have all the current aspects of the book in mind when I began this effort. The fundamental need to embed positive values and virtuousness within an organization became evident over time, as described in Chapter 5. The idea that 'efficiencyism' was holding organizations back was an outgrowth of a paper presentation I heard at the Academy of Management annual meeting in 2015 (referenced in Chapter 1).

Chapters 7 & 13 of the book started life as part of a paper that I presented to the annual meeting of the Academy of Management (AOM) in 2015, Vancouver, BC (C. G. Chandler 2015). Several anonymous AOM reviewers provided useful comments that were important to my later efforts.

Many of the remaining chapters of the book grew out of episodes of my podcast (The Age of Organizational Effectiveness), which can be accessed at www.AgeofOE. com (or at other outlets where podcasts are found).

I am grateful to the early readers of the draft manuscript, including Linda Chandler, Chaz Chandler, F. Tomasson (Tom) Jannuzi, and Robert Kluting. Their comments encouraged my subsequent efforts, and were instrumental in deciding the direction to undertake when revisions were necessary. Any deficiencies are my own.

My publisher has been important to the success of this effort, particularly Kary Oberbrunner and David Branderhorst who provide the driving force behind Author Academy Elite. I would recommend them to other authors in search of a home. Many thanks to Chris O'Byrne of Jet-Launch for managing the book's interior design. Finally, the book's cover art was created through 99Designs.

Connect with me at www.BecomeTrulyGreat.com, or on social media at LinkedIn.

Charles G. Chandler, Ph.D.

INDEX